NORMAN LEWIS

JAMES BROOKS

ROBERT ARNESON

DAVID SMITH

HAROLD COUSINS

CHARLES ALSTON

ARLES SELIGER

THEODOROS STAMOS

ONRAD MARCA-RELLI

HARD POUSETTE-DART

RICHARD HUNT

URGEOIS

MILTON RESNICK

COU

CLAIRE FALKENSTEIN

SEYMOUR LIPTON

HALE WOODRUFF

RICHARD STANKIEWICZ

ALMA THOMAS

EFEO

K TOBEY

CHARLES ALSTON

ROBERT ARNESON

NORMAN BLUHM

LEE BONTECOU

LOUISE BOURGEOIS

JAMES BROOKS

JOHN CHAMBERLAIN

HAROLD COUSINS

JAY DEFEO

DOROTHY DEHNER

BEAUFORD DELANEY

CLAIRE FALKENSTEIN

HERBERT FERBER

DAVID HARE

HANS HOFMANN

RICHARD HUNT

LEE KRASNER

IBRAM LASSAW

ALFRED LESLIE

NORMAN LEWIS

SEYMOUR LIPTON

CONRAD MARCA-RELLI

JOHN MASON

JOAN MITCHELL

LOUISE NEVELSON

ALFONSO OSSORIO

RICHARD POUSETTE-DART

MILTON RESNICK

THEODORE ROSZAK

CHARLES SELIGER

DAVID SMITH

THEODOROS STAMOS

RICHARD STANKIEWICZ

TOSHIKO TAKAEZU

ALMA THOMAS

MARK TOBEY

JACK TWORKOV

PETER VOULKOS

HALE WOODRUFF

ABSTRACT EXPRESSIONISM

FURTHER EVIDENCE

PAINTING & SCULPTURE

MICHAEL ROSENFELD GALLERY, LLC

NEW YORK

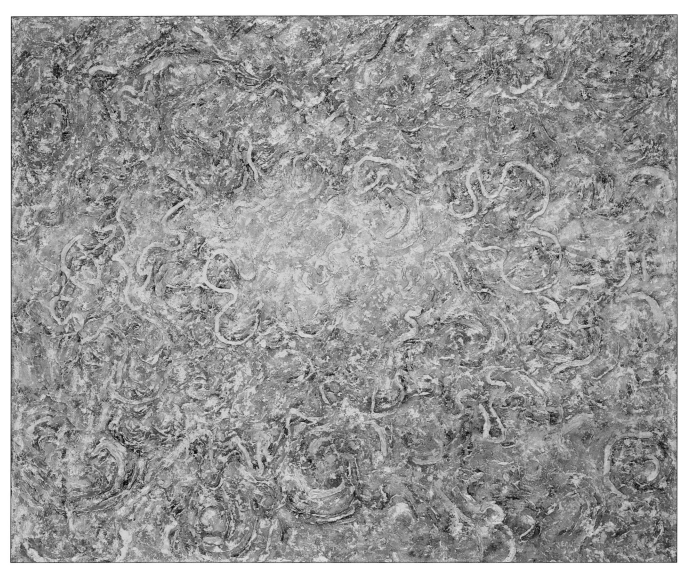

BEAUFORD DELANEY (1901-1979), *COMPOSITION 16*, 1954-56, OIL ON CANVAS, 31 1/2 X 36 7/8 INCHES, SIGNED

ABSTRACT EXPRESSIONISM

THE FORTY-YEAR-OLD TERMS, ABSTRACT AND SURREALIST, ARE CINDERELLA SLIPPERS, AND THERE'S NO USE PRETENDING THEY FIT ALL OF THE NEW GENERATION.

— EDWARD ALDEN JEWELL, 1943

Edward Alden Jewell, "The Realm of Art: A New Platform; 'Globalism' Pops into View," *New York Times,* June 13, 1943. Reprinted in Ellen G. Landau, ed., *Reading Abstract Expressionism: Context and Critique* (New Haven: Yale University Press, 2005), 152-153.

CLASSIFICATION IS EXTRANEOUS TO ART. MOST LABELS ATTACHED TO PAINTING ARE UNENLIGHTENING. TALENTS THE THING. "ISMS" ARE LITERATURE. NEVERTHELESS, A LARGE PART OF THE PUBLIC THAT LOOKS AT CONTEMPORARY PAINTING DEMANDS CLASSIFICATION. . . .

DURING THE PAST DOZEN YEARS, AND PARTICULARLY SINCE 1940, THE TENDENCY TOWARD A NEW METAMORPHISM WAS MANIFEST IN PAINTING. HOWEVER THIS MAY SEEM RELATED WITH TOTEMIC IMAGES, EARLIEST MEDITERRANEAN ART AND OTHER ARCHAIC MATERIAL, IT DOES NOT, IN RE-EXAMINATION, APPEAR TO UTILIZE ANY OF THESE FOR DIRECT INSPIRATIONAL SOURCES. ONE DISCOVERS THAT THE REAL FORERUNNERS OF THE NEW "ISM" WERE ARP AND MIRÓ, . . .

HERE THE NEW "ISM" FINDS ITS MOST EFFECTIVE SUPPORT AMONG AMERICAN PAINTERS. THE CLOSENESS OF OBJECTIVE RESEMBLANCE TO PRE-COLUMBIAN EXPRESSIONS INDIGENOUS TO THIS HEMISPHERE IS AN INCIDENTAL FACTOR. WHAT COUNTS IS THAT THE PAINTERS, HOWEVER RESPECTFUL, ARE UNIMPRESSED WITH ANY IDEA OF BECOMING "ANOTHER PICASSO" OR "ANOTHER MIRÓ," AND THAT THEIR WORKS INDICATE GENUINE TALENT, ENTHUSIASM AND ORIGINALITY. I BELIEVE WE SEE REAL AMERICAN PAINTING BEGINNING NOW.

—HOWARD PUTZEL, 1945

Howard Putzel, "A Problem for Critics," Ellen G. Landau, ed., *Reading Abstract Expressionism: Context and Critique* (New Haven: Yale University Press, 2005), 152-153.

ALFRED LESLIE (B.1927), *UNTITLED*, 1954, OIL AND COLLAGE ON CANVAS, 7 1/4 X 7 INCHES, SIGNED

*T*HEIR PAINTINGS STARTLE BECAUSE, TO THE UNINITIATED EYE, THEY APPEAR TO RELY SO MUCH ON ACCIDENT, WHIM, AND HAPHAZARD EFFECT. AN UNGOVERNED SPONTANEITY SEEMS TO BE AT PLAY, INTENT ONLY ON REGISTERING IMMEDIATE IMPULSE, AND THE RESULT SEEMS TO BE NOTHING MORE THAN A WELTER OF BLURS, BLOTCHES, AND SCRAWLS—"OLEAGINOUS" AND "AMORPHOUS" AS ONE BRITISH CRITIC DESCRIBED IT. ALL THIS IS SEEMING. THERE IS GOOD AND BAD IN ABSTRACT EXPRESSIONISM, AND ONCE ONE CAN TELL THE DIFFERENCE, HE DISCOVERS THAT THE GOOD OWES ITS REALIZATION TO A SEVERER DISCIPLINE THAT CAN BE FOUND ELSEWHERE IN CONTEMPORARY PAINTING; ONLY IT MAKES FACTORS EXPLICIT THAT PREVIOUS DISCIPLINES LEFT IMPLICIT, AND LEAVES IMPLICIT MANY THAT THEY DID NOT.

— CLEMENT GREENBERG, 1955

Clement Greenberg, "American-Type Painting," *Partisan Review* (Spring 1955), 179-96. Reprinted in Ellen G. Landau, ed., *Reading Abstract Expressionism: Context and Critique* (New Haven: Yale University Press, 2005), 199-200.

*U*PON ENTERING THE ROOM, A STRANGE SENSATION LIKE THAT OF MAGNETIC TENSION SURROUNDS YOU, AS THOUGH THE EXPRESSION CONCENTRATED IN THE CANVASES WOULD SPRING FROM THEM. THEY ARE OTHER MYTHS, OTHER GODS, OTHER IDEAS, DIFFERENT FROM THOSE PREVAILING IN EUROPE AT PRESENT. . . . EACH PICTURE IS A CONFESSION, AN INTIMATE CHAT WITH THE DIVINITY, ACCEPTING OR DENYING THE EXTERIOR WORLD BUT ALWAYS FAITHFUL TO THE MORE PROFOUND IDENTITY OF CONSCIENCE.

—MERCEDES MOLLEDA, 1958

Mercedes Molleda, Revista, Barcelona, August 30, 1958 (review of *The New American Painting* exhibition curated by Alfred H. Barr, Jr.). Reprinted in Ellen G. Landau, ed., *Reading Abstract Expressionism: Context and Critique* (New Haven: Yale University Press, 2005), 220.

*A*T A CERTAIN MOMENT, THE CANVAS BEGAN TO APPEAR TO ONE AMERICAN PAINTER AFTER ANOTHER AS AN ARENA IN WHICH TO ACT—RATHER THAN AS A SPACE IN WHICH TO REPRODUCE, RE-DESIGN, ANALYZE OR "EXPRESS" AN OBJECT, ACTUAL OR IMAGINED. WHAT WAS TO GO ON THE CANVAS WAS NOT A PICTURE BUT AN EVENT. THE PAINTER NO LONGER APPROACHED HIS EASEL WITH AN IMAGE IN HIS MIND; HE WENT UP TO IT WITH MATERIAL IN HIS HAND TO DO SOMETHING TO THAT OTHER PIECE OF MATERIAL IN FRONT OF HIM. THE IMAGE WOULD BE THE RESULT OF THIS ENCOUNTER.

—HAROLD ROSENBERG, 1959

Harold Rosenberg, *The Tradition of the New* (New York: Horizon Press, 1959), 25. Quoted in Helen Gardner, Fred S. Kleiner, Christin J. Mamiya, *Gardner's Art Through the Ages: The Western Perspective* (Cengage Learning, 2005), 813.

PART ONE: PAINTING

MARCH 14 – JULY 31, 2009

MICHAEL ROSENFELD GALLERY, LLC
NEW YORK, NY

I'M INTENSELY INTERESTED IN SPACE, FORM, COLOR, THE THINGS THAT CHALLENGE ALL CONTEMPORARY ARTISTS. IT WOULD BE WONDERFUL IF I COULD JUST SIT BACK AND DO IT ESTHETICALLY. BUT I HAVE TO REACT TO THE OTHER THING. I'M PART OF IT, I HAVE NO CHOICE. I THINK I'VE GOTTEN TO THE POINT WHERE IT ISN'T SATISFYING TO DO ANOTHER HANDSOME, DECORATIVE ABSTRACTION. PAINTING HAS BECOME SO IMPERSONAL. I HAVE A NEED TO RELATE TO HUMANITY IN A MORE DIRECT WAY.[*]

CHARLES ALSTON 1907-1977

Charles Alston was born in Charlotte, North Carolina in 1907 to the Reverend Primus Priss Alston and Anna Elizabeth Miller Alston. Alston's father, who nicknamed him Spinky, died when Alston was three. His mother subsequently married Harry Bearden, uncle of Romare Bearden. In 1915, the family moved to Harlem, but Alston continued to spend summers in North Carolina until he was fifteen. As a teenager, Alston painted and sculpted from life, mastering an academic-realist style, and in 1925, he was offered a scholarship to the Yale School of Fine Arts, but attended Columbia University instead. In 1929, Alston received his BA with a concentration in fine arts, and decided to continue on for a master's degree at Columbia University Teachers College, where he became increasingly interested in African art and aesthetics. While in graduate school, he taught at the Utopia Children's House, where he became a mentor to Jacob Lawrence. After receiving his MA in 1931, Alston continued to work in the Harlem community, co-founding the Harlem Art Workshop in 1934. When the Workshop needed more space, he found it at 306 West 141st Street. Aided by funding from the Works Progress Administration (WPA), "306" (as it was known) became a center for the most creative minds in Harlem; regulars included Bearden, Lawrence, Augusta Savage, Richard Wright, Robert Blackburn, Countee Cullen, Ralph Ellison, and Gwendolyn Knight. In 1935, Alston became the first black supervisor in the Federal Art Project when he was assigned to direct the WPA's Harlem Hospital murals. The paintings he designed—influenced by the work of Mexican muralists, jazz music, and the prevailing social realism of the 1930s—were approved by the Federal Art Project but rejected by the hospital's administration for what they saw as an excess of subject matter relating to African Americans. After protests and extensive press coverage, the muralists were allowed to proceed. In 1936, two of the works were exhibited at the Museum of Modern Art, New York (MoMA). Two Rosenwald Fellowships at the end of the decade enabled Alston to travel throughout the south and to work with Hale Woodruff at Atlanta University.

During World War II, Alston worked as an artist for the Office of War Information, served in the US Army, and was also a member of the board of directors for the National Mural Society. In 1944, he attended the Pratt Institute in Brooklyn for a year, and in 1949, he and Woodruff created murals for the Golden State Mutual Life Insurance building in Los Angeles. Entitled *Negro in California History*, the project comprised two works—*Exploration and Colonization (1537-1850)* by Alston and *Settlement and Development (1850-1949)* by Woodruff.

Alston began creating abstract paintings in the 1950s, but he never abandoned figural representation. Instead, he would shift between the two modes of painting, depending on what he believed was best for a given subject. In 1950, he entered one of his new, abstract works in the competitive exhibition *American Painting Today* at the Metropolitan Museum of Art. It won the purchase prize, and the museum acquired it. Many of Alston's abstract works from this decade are inspired by African art, but unlike the abstract expressionist passion for American Indian, Pacific, and African art—all of which they grouped together under the generic label of "primitive"— Alston's paintings are created through an intimate knowledge of African aesthetics. In Alston's work, the African influence is part of a dialogue between past and present, one that finds modernism in tradition and vice-versa.

From his early days at the Utopia Children's House in 1930 until his death in 1977, Alston remained an influential teacher and a committed activist. He taught at the Art Students League, MoMA, and City College. In 1963, he co-founded the Spiral Group (along with Romare Bearden, Norman Lewis, Hale Woodruff, and others) in order to increase gallery and museum representation for black artists. In 1967, President Lyndon Johnson appointed Alston as a trustee of the Kennedy Center, and in 1970, Alston became a member of the New York City Arts Commission. In 1975, Columbia University Teacher's College, which once barred Alston from a required life-drawing course because the models were white, honored him with its first Distinguished Alumni Award.

* Grace Glueck, "Art Notes: 'The Best Painter I Can Possibly Be,'" *New York Times*, Dec. 8, 1968.

CHARLES ALSTON (1907-1977), *UNTITLED*, 1961, OIL ON CANVAS, 50 X 30 INCHES, SIGNED

THE VIOLENCE IN MY '60S PAINTINGS WAS THERE BECAUSE THE VIOLENCE EXIST-
ED IN THE MAN HIMSELF. AT THAT PERIOD IN MY LIFE I WAS ALWAYS CAUSING
TROUBLE. THE GESTURE WAS PART OF THAT VIOLENCE. I MEAN, IF YOU HIT A CAN-
VAS WITH A BIG BRUSH WITH A LOT OF PAINT ON IT, YOU'RE GOING TO CREATE AN
ATMOSPHERE OF VIOLENCE, AND THAT'S WHAT I DID THEN. I DO NOT HAVE THAT
OUTLOOK NOW.*

NORMAN BLUHM

1921-1999

Born in 1921, **Norman Bluhm** grew up on Chicago's South Side and in Lucca, Italy, where his mother's family lived. An advanced student, Bluhm completed high school with honors when he was sixteen, and from 1936 to 1941, he studied architecture at the Armour Institute of Technology (later Illinois Institute of Technology) with Mies van der Rohe. When the United States entered World War II, Bluhm enlisted and became a B-26 pilot. The war had a profound effect on Bluhm's life and psyche—he had been injured, and his younger brother, also a pilot, was killed. Although afterwards Bluhm attempted to resume his studies at the Armour Institute, he had lost interest in architecture and found it difficult to fall back into his old life. In 1947, against the wishes of his family, Bluhm decided to become an artist. He moved to Paris and studied at the Ecole des Beaux-Arts and the Académie de la Grande Chaumière with funding from the GI Bill. In Paris, Bluhm met other American abstractionists such as Joan Mitchell and Sam Francis, as well as members of Europe's artistic and intellectual avant-garde, including Jean Cocteau, Antonin Artaud, and Alberto Giacometti. During the nine years he spent in Europe, Bluhm's artwork moved away from his initial landscapes inspired by Cézanne and towards abstraction. Although Bluhm lived an ocean away from the epicenter of abstract expressionism, his works of the early 1950s share its gestural brushstrokes, visible paint drips, and pulsating color. When Bluhm returned to the United States in 1956, he settled in New York, where he joined Franz Kline, Robert Motherwell, Ad Reinhardt, Willem de Kooning, and others as a member of the Club—the group of artists, writers, and art dealers who would meet in an apartment at 39 East 8th Street—and became a regular at the Cedar Bar. A year after his arrival in the New York art world, Bluhm had his first U.S. solo exhibition, at the Leo Castelli Gallery.

Bluhm acknowledged his artistic debt to artists of the New York School, but he also rejected the label of "second-generation abstract expressionist," which he saw as limiting and pejorative. While his work of the 1950s and 1960s shares the aesthetic and conceptual concerns of abstract expressionism, Bluhm had also begun to test the limits of this particular approach to painting, most notably in the "poem-paintings" he created in collaboration with Frank O'Hara. Poet, curator, and ardent supporter of abstract expressionist art, O'Hara was also a friend of Bluhm's and had included his work in a selection of artists for Documenta II in 1959. In 1961, they created twenty-six improvisational works that brought together words, letters, and brushstrokes—experiments in linguistic as well as visual abstraction. In the 1970s, Bluhm's style underwent another significant transformation. His work grew in scale and featured lush, curvaceous shapes suggestive of female forms, rendered in bright blues, warm pink and purple tones, and hot reds. Titles such as *Arethusa*, *Mermaid's Delight*, and *Guillotine Lady* strengthen the works' associations to the feminine. Bluhm continued to expand the size of his works throughout his career. By the 1980s and 1990s, he was creating a single image across three canvases. In addition to their art historical overtones, these triptychs also served a practical function—they enabled Bluhm to work on a mythical scale and still fit his paintings through his studio door.

Bluhm enjoyed a steady level of success and critical acclaim throughout his career as an artist, although his relationship to the New York art world was fraught with ambivalence. Disturbed by what he saw as a growing commercialization of art, Bluhm left the city for Millbrook, New York in 1970. He later moved to East Hampton and then settled in Vermont in 1986. Bluhm continued to exhibit in Europe throughout his life, and his work has consistently found support among artists and critics alike.

* John Yau and Jonathan Gams, "26 Things at Once: An Interview with Norman Bluhm," http://www.culturereport.com/culturereport/artists/bluhm/index.html (accessed February 2009).

NORMAN BLUHM (1921-1999), *WHITE EYE*, 1958, OIL ON CANVAS, 36 1/2 X 44 INCHES, SIGNED

NORMAN BLUHM (1921-1999), *FALLEN MONUMENT*, 1960, OIL ON CANVAS, 72 X 48 INCHES, SIGNED

MY PAINTING STARTS WITH A COMPLICATION ON THE CANVAS SURFACE, DONE WITH AS MUCH SPONTANEITY AND AS LITTLE MEMORY AS POSSIBLE. THIS THEN EXISTS AS THE SUBJECT. IT IS AS STRANGE AS A NEW STILL LIFE ARRANGEMENT AS CONFUSING AS ANY UNFAMILIAR SITUATION. IT DEMANDS A LONG PERIOD OF ACQUAINTANCE DURING WHICH IT IS OBSERVED BOTH INNOCENTLY AND SHREWDLY. THEN IT SPEAKS, QUIETLY, WITH ITS OWN PECULIAR LOGIC. BETWEEN PAINTING AND PAINTER A DIALOGUE DEVELOPS, WHICH LEADS RAPIDLY TO THE BARE CONFRONTATION OF TWO PERSONALITIES.*

James Brooks

1906-1992

Born in St. Louis, Missouri in 1906, **James Brooks** spent his childhood in Colorado, Oklahoma, Illinois, and Texas, due to his father's occupation as a traveling salesman. Brooks began drawing at a young age, finding his inspiration in comic strips and magazines. In the early 1920s, he studied at Southern Methodist University and the Dallas Art Institute. In 1926, Brooks left school to go to New York, where he studied at the Grand Central Art School with the illustrator Pruett Carter. Given his lack of exposure to art museums as a child, Brooks had never distinguished illustration from fine art before arriving in New York. When he began to see a difference, he lost interest in illustration, and left Grand Central to study with Kimon Nicolaides and Boardman Robinson at the Art Students League. To support himself, Brooks worked as a commercial artist, doing lettering. In the 1930s, with encouragement from Burgoyne Diller, Brooks joined the Federal Art Project of the WPA, where he met Jackson Pollock and Philip Guston. Like many WPA artists, Brooks was also a member of the Artists Union, which was organized to protect the rights of artists and workers. He created several murals for the WPA, including his famous Flight at the old rotunda of LaGuardia Airport's Marine Air Terminal. Although the Port Authority painted over the mural in the 1950s, the work was restored roughly thirty years later. In 1942, Brooks joined the army. After the war, he returned to New York and began teaching art, first at Columbia University and then at the Pratt Institute.

In the late 1940s, Brooks turned away from his figural, Orozco-inspired social realism of the Depression and war years, and towards abstraction. Like Pollock and other abstract expressionists, Brooks was not content simply to find a new artistic voice; he wanted to dismantle approaches to painting that had become ingrained. An accidental discovery in 1947 inspired Brooks to develop a new method—after gluing a series of drawings onto Bemis cloth, Brooks noticed that the glue had seeped through the cloth, forming provocative shapes on the other side. He began staining his canvases and using the spontaneous splash of color as a foundation for a more deliberate painting. Building an abstract composition out of a quasi-accidental moment, Brooks conceptualized painting as "a chain of formal reactions." In 1950, Brooks had his first solo show, at the Peridot Gallery in New York. The following year, he helped organize and participated in the famous *Ninth Street Show*, which also included work by Pollock, Kline, de Kooning, Motherwell, and Hans Hofmann. Brooks's masterful compositions featuring rhythmic arrangements of color, space, and shape earned him praise from critics as well as a place in two of MoMA's most prestigious mid-century exhibitions: *Twelve Americans* (1956) and *New American Painting,* which was organized by MoMA's International Program in 1958 and traveled throughout Europe. In 1963, the Whitney Museum of American Art mounted a traveling, mid-career retrospective of Brooks's work.

Brooks's paintings shift and vibrate with fields of color. Although he shared with his fellow abstract expressionists an interest in spontaneity, controlled accidents, and action painting, he was less urgently invested in creating mythic painting or using art as a trance-like path to his unconscious. Instead, Brooks was primarily invested in analyzing the formal structure of art, and his willingness to experiment with a smaller scale led him to create dense, powerful works that rival his large canvases in their adroit handling of form, line, and color. Throughout the remainder of his career, Brooks continued to received honors and awards, including a Guggenheim Fellowship (1969) and a grant from the National Endowment for the Arts (1973).

* James Brooks, "Catalogue Statement for the University of Illinois, 1951," reprinted on artnet: http://www.artnet.com/awc/james-brooks.html (accessed February 2009).

JAMES BROOKS (1906-1992), *#37-1951,* 1951, OIL ON CANVAS, 36 X 68 INCHES, SIGNED

JAMES BROOKS (1906-1992), *E-1954*, 1954, OIL ON CANVAS, 31 1/2 INCHES (DIAMETER), SIGNED

I REGARD MYSELF AS AN EXPRESSIONIST AS WELL AS A SYMBOLIST. IF EXPRESSION-
ISM IMPLIES EMOTIONAL IMPACT, I CAN REALIZE IT ONLY BY RESTRAINT AND ULTI-
MATE REFINEMENT.*

 1929-1989

Emerging with the abstract expressionist movement, **Jay DeFeo** worked for four decades as a sculptor, photographer and painter, producing a broad and personal vocabulary of heroic imagery that was inspired by ordinary objects and influenced by prehistoric art,
astronomy, and architecture. Labeled an abstract expressionist, "Beat painter," and "symbolist," she was born "Mary Joan" in 1929 in
Hanover, New Hampshire and raised in San Francisco, rural northern California, and Colorado. She received her introduction to art from
a neighbor who lent her a "how to draw" book that exposed her to the design principles and basic geometric forms that would later
dominate her art. In 1946, she attended the University of California at Berkeley, where she earned both her BA and MA degrees in studio art. Awarded the Sigmund Martin Heller Traveling Fellowship in 1951, the first woman to be honored with this distinguished prize,
DeFeo spent eighteen months traveling in Europe, exploring Paris, London, and Florence. During this time, she painted prolifically, working quickly through various art historical styles and arriving at abstract expressionism. Upon her return to the United States, DeFeo settled in the San Francisco Bay Area, where she became a central figure in the California avant-garde, along with friends Bruce Conner,
Joan Brown, George Herms, and Wallace Berman.

In 1958, DeFeo began construction of her legendary painting The Rose (now in the collection of the Whitney Museum of American Art,
New York). Over the course of seven years, she built up the surface of the painting using a mixture of oil, primer, and mica to create an
abstract, topographical landscape at the center of which was a beaming, white focal point rising eight inches above the surface of the
canvas. By the time she lost the lease to her Fillmore Street studio and had to move, the eight-by-ten-foot painting was too heavy to
carry, and it had to be removed through her studio window with a forklift, an event documented by Conner in his film The White Rose.
DeFeo spent the rest of the decade recovering from the emotional and physical exhaustion caused by both the painting and the end of
her marriage. When she began to work again in 1970, DeFeo produced a body of drawings, photographs, photo-collages and paintings
that often focused on single, inanimate objects. She deliberately distorted and mystified the tripods, goggles, and teeth she depicted,
transforming them into magical, provocative forms executed in shades of black and white.

For DeFeo, a self-proclaimed formalist, the process of making art was "an exploration, an experimentation, and a sheer love of materials"
that, like her life, was an "additive and subtractive, a constructive and deconstructive process." She had her first solo exhibition in 1954 at
the Place, a tavern and Beat poet hangout in San Francisco's North Beach, before exhibiting at the legendary Ferus Gallery in Los Angeles
in 1960. Throughout her life, DeFeo was an influential teacher—first at the San Francisco Art Institute and the California College of Arts
and Crafts, and during the 1980s, at Mills College. Although the work of Jay DeFeo has been exhibited consistently over the years, main-
ly on the West Coast, her inclusion in the 1995 exhibition *Beat Culture and the New America: 1950-1965* at the Whitney redefined her sig-
nificance within the history of twentieth-century American art and prompted a reexamination of her entire life's oeuvre.

* Jay DeFeo, catalogue statement, "Sixteen Americans," Museum of Modern Art, New York, 1959. Quoted on http://www.jaydefeo.org/paint.html (accessed July 2009).

JAY DEFEO (1929-1989), *UNTITLED (FLORENCE)*, 1952, TEMPERA AND SILVER PIGMENT ON PAPER, 26 1/2 X 19 1/2 INCHES

THE ABSTRACTION OSTENSIBLY, IS SIMPLY FOR ME A PENETRATION OF SOMETHING THAT IS MORE PROFOUND IN MANY WAYS THAN THE RIGIDITY OF FORM. A FORM IF IT BREATHES SOME, IF IT HAS SOME ENIGMA TO IT, IT IS ALSO THE ENIGMA THAT IS THE ABSTRACT. I WOULD THINK.*

BEAUFORD DELANEY

1901-1979

Known for his lyrical abstractions of color and light, **Beauford Delaney** was born in Knoxville, Tennessee in 1901, the eighth of ten children. His mother, Delia, had been born into slavery in 1865 and was a devout Christian who imparted her strict beliefs on her children. His father, John Samuel Delaney, was a Methodist Episcopal preacher. When he was fifteen, Delaney met local artist Lloyd Branson, a white painter who gave Delaney art lessons in exchange for his doing odd jobs around the studio. But Delaney's relatively peaceful life was also marked by tragedy from an early age. In 1915, his sister and best friend, Ogust Mae, died, and in 1919 the death of his father coincided with the Knoxville race riot that accompanied the brutal lynching of Maurice Hayes. These events traumatized him and haunted his psyche throughout his life. In 1923, Delaney left Knoxville for Boston, where he studied art at the Massachusetts Normal School (later the Massachusetts College of Art), the Copley Society, and the South Boston School of Art. In 1929, he moved to New York City and studied for a brief time at the Art Students League with John Sloan and Thomas Hart Benton. He joined the Federal Art Project of the WPA and in 1935 became part of the team of artists chosen to work on Charles Alston's Harlem Hospital murals.

Although he frequented 306 and was a member of the Harlem Artists Guild, Delaney was consumed by his own artistic vision. He was firmly connected to the Greenwich Village community, and he exhibited regularly at Michael Freilich's RoKo Gallery. His paintings of the 1940s and early 1950s consisted largely of portraits, modernist interiors, and street scenes executed in impasto with broad areas of vibrant colors. His interest in the arts included poetry and jazz, and he formed close friendships with writers such as James Baldwin and Henry Miller, and artists including Alfred Stieglitz, Georgia O'Keefe, and Al Hirschfeld. Delaney moved through the circles of both black and white artists and intellectuals in New York with relative ease, but he was also nagged by constant feelings of marginalization, along the lines race, class, and also sexuality.

In 1953, Delaney left New York and traveled to Europe, settling in Paris. Feeling a new sense of freedom from racial and sexual biases, he focused on creating lyrical, colorful, non-objective abstractions. These paintings, consisting of elaborate and fluid swirls of paint applied in luminous hues, were pure and simplified expressions of light. Although the paintings have clear ties to Monet's studies of light, Delaney's works are expressionistic rather than impressionistic. The light Delaney sought to capture was not the actual light of day, but a transcendent, eternal, spiritual light. Sadly, the optimism in these stunning works was not enough to protect Delaney from despair, and in 1961, he attempted suicide. With financial help from friends, including Baldwin, Miller, and painter Lawrence Calcagno, Delaney was hospitalized in 1962. Afterwards, he created a series of works he called his Rorschach tests, paintings where light is "enshrouded or overwhelmed, struggling to hold the forces of darkness at bay."† In 1978, the Studio Museum in Harlem organized his first major retrospective exhibition, and a year later, Delaney died in Paris while hospitalized for mental illness.

* Richard Long interview with Beauford Delaney, September 5, 1970.
† Joyce Henri Robinson, An Artistic Friendship: Beauford Delaney and Lawrence Calcagno (Penn State Press, 2001), 13.

BEAUFORD DELANEY (1901-1979), *UNTITLED*, C.1954, OIL ON CANVAS, 59 X 23 1/4 INCHES, SIGNED

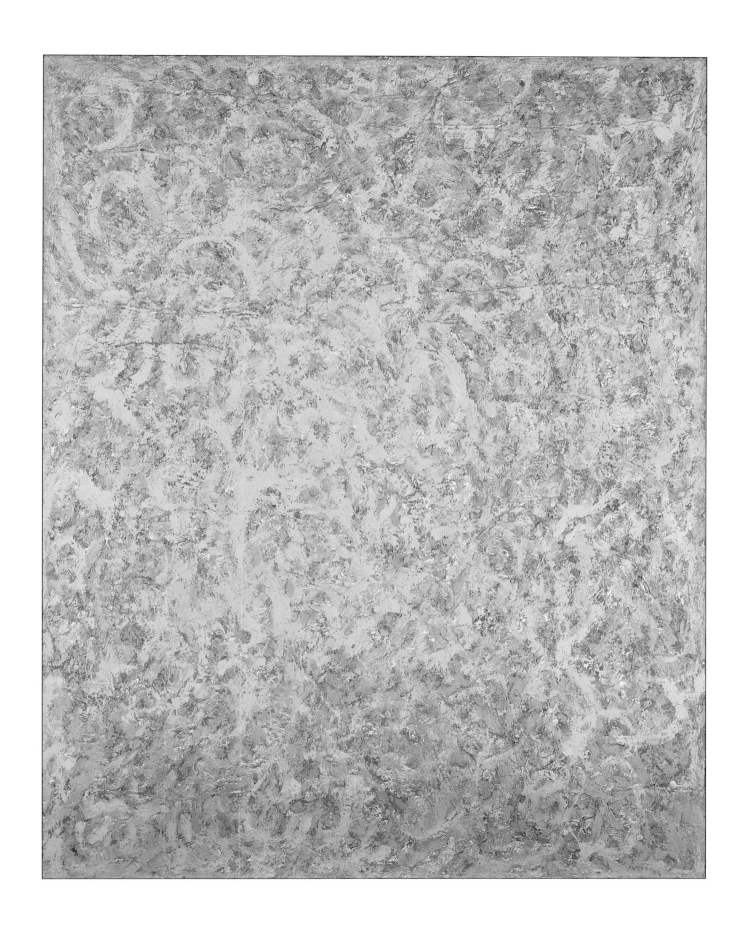

THE MAGIC OF PAINTING . . . CAN NEVER BE FULLY, RATIONALLY EXPLAINED. IT IS THE HARMONY OF HEART AND MIND IN THE CAPACITY OF FEELING INTO THINGS THAT PLAYS THE INSTRUMENT. THE INSTRUMENT ANSWERS THE THROB OF THE HEART IN EVERY INSTANCE. PAINTING IS ALWAYS INTUITIVELY CONDITIONED. . . . PICTORIAL LIFE IS NOT IMITATED LIFE; IT IS, ON THE CONTRARY, A CREATED REALITY BASED ON THE INHERENT LIFE WITHIN EVERY MEDIUM OF EXPRESSION. WE HAVE ONLY TO AWAKEN IT.*

. . . [HANS HOFMANN] IS CERTAINLY ONE OF THE MOST UNCOMPROMISING REPRESENTATIVES OF WHAT SOME PEOPLE CALL THE SPATTER-AND-DAUB SCHOOL OF PAINTING AND I, MORE POLITELY, HAVE CHRISTENED ABSTRACT EXPRESSIONISM....†

Hans Hofmann 1880-1966

Born in Germany in 1880, **Hans Hofmann** was by far the oldest of the abstract expressionists, although his artwork of the 1950s and 1960s contains a youthful exuberance that is balanced by a masterful understanding of color's expressive and formal potential. In Europe, Hofmann was a respected teacher and painter. In 1904, he studied at the Académie Colarossi and the Académie de la Grande Chaumière in Paris, where he met Picasso, Georges Braque, and Henri Matisse. In Germany, he exhibited with the Neue Sezession and the Paul Cassirer Gallery in Berlin before settling in Munich and opening an art school in 1915, the Schule für Bildes Kunst, which acquired an international reputation in the years following World War I. In 1930, Worth Ryder, a former student of Hofmann's and a professor at the University of California, Berkeley, invited Hofmann to teach a summer session. Hofmann returned to the United States the following year, and in 1932, he decided to stay in the country given the rising hostility in Germany towards artists and intellectuals. Hofmann settled in New York, where he procured a teaching position at the Art Students League with the help of Vaclav Vytlacil. In 1934, he opened the Hofmann School of Fine Art at 137 East 57th Street in New York. From its inception, the Hofmann School (which moved to 52 West Eighth Street in 1938) taught an impressive list of students, including, Frank Stella, Wolf Kahn, Lee Krasner, Red Grooms, and Helen Frankenthaler. In 1935, Hofmann also opened a summer school in Provincetown, Massachusetts.

An enthusiastic and admired teacher, Hofmann was a respected painter throughout his career. In 1941, the year he became a U.S. citizen, Hofmann had a solo exhibition at the Isaac Delgado Museum of Art in New Orleans. His first New York show was at Peggy Guggenheim's Art of this Century Gallery in 1944. The following year, the Whitney mounted *Contemporary American Painting,* which included work by Hofmann. In 1947, Hofmann found a permanent home at Kootz Gallery, New York, which held exhibitions of his work almost yearly until his death. He also continued to exhibit in Europe at such venues as the Galerie Maeght, Paris—whose owners would later establish the prestigious Maeght Foundation in Saint-Paul, France.

Hofmann flourished in the 1950s and 1960s with large canvases that dazzled in their bold planes of invigorating colors. He joined the "Irascibles" in protest against the Met's exclusion of avant-garde artwork from its juried exhibitions, and he was also part of the Studio 35 three-day symposium on abstract art, which included—among others—Norman Lewis, James Brooks, Theodoros Stamos, and Willem de Kooning. In 1957, the Whitney organized a traveling retrospective of Hofmann's work, and the following year, Hofmann closed his art school in order to devote all of his energy to painting. The closing of the Hofmann School brought an end to what had been an important institution for the history of American abstraction, and Hofmann's contribution as an artist-teacher was recognized in the traveling exhibition *Hans Hofmann and His Students,* organized by William Seitz for MoMA in 1963. Three honorary doctorates in fine art—from Dartmouth College (1962), UC Berkeley (1963), and the Pratt Institute (1965)—also testify to the many artists whose work was enriched by Hofmann and his extraordinary painting.

* Hans Hofmann, "The Color Problem in Pure Painting—Its Creative Origin," first published in *Hans Hofmann: New Paintings,* exh. cat. (New York: Kootz Gallery, 1955). Reprinted in Helmut Friedel and Tina Dickey, *Hans Hofmann* (Manchester, Vermont: Hudson Hills Press, 1998), 12. http://books.google.com/books?id=VqhNCxKU-D4C&dq (accessed July 2009).

† Robert Coates, "The Art Galleries: Abroad and at Home," *The New Yorker,* March 30, 1946, 83.

HANS HOFMANN (1880-1966). *COMPOSITION NO. 9.* 1953. OIL ON CANVAS, 38 X 30 INCHES, SIGNED

I NEVER VIOLATE AN INNER RHYTHM. I LOATHE TO FORCE ANYTHING. I DON'T KNOW
IF THE INNER RHYTHM IS EASTERN OR WESTERN. I KNOW IT IS ESSENTIAL FOR ME.
I LISTEN TO IT AND I STAY WITH IT. I HAVE ALWAYS BEEN THIS WAY. I HAVE REGARDS
FOR THE INNER VOICE.*

*L*EE *K*RASNER   1908-1984

Lee Krasner was born Lena Krassner in 1908 to parents who had emigrated from Russia to Brooklyn. In 1928, she studied at the Art Students League, and in 1929, after graduating from the Women's Art School of Cooper Union, she enrolled in classes at the National Academy of Design, where she studied until 1932. Although Krasner received excellent technical training at the Academy, she found the conservative atmosphere stifling, and she was often in conflict with her teachers. Krasner continued her education afterwards, taking courses at City College while supporting herself as a model and waitress. In 1934, she joined the Federal Art Project of the WPA and became a member of the Artists Union. In addition to her work with the WPA, Krasner decided to study with Hans Hofmann from 1937 to 1940. At the Hofmann School of Art, Krasner was encouraged to jettison the naturalist tendencies she had acquired through earlier schooling, and she quickly developed an abstract vocabulary, producing cubist-inspired compositions that featured bold geometric forms outlined in black and filled with bright colors. In the 1940s, Krasner pursued her interest in abstraction further, joining the American Abstract Artists (AAA), with whom she exhibited regularly. Although she had met Jackson Pollock briefly in 1936, they did not get to know each other until 1941, when Krasner arrived at his studio to see the work of this AAA member with whom she was unfamiliar. His paintings impressed her, and the two artists began a romantic relationship. In 1945, they married and moved to East Hampton.

Pollock's art and methods of working had a profound affect on Krasner, but his influence never obscured her own vision, nor did it go unreciprocated. As Pollock's work increased in scale, Krasner devised a different approach to freeing herself from easel painting. In 1945, she began her "Little Image" works, "intimate paintings, rich in surface texture, often loosely structured in a grid yet full of energy and improvisation," and featuring calligraphic forms.[†] Krasner's mastery of composition—of a painting's structure—had an important impact on Pollock's artwork, as did her maturity as an artist, a trait evident in her willingness to reevaluate and rework earlier paintings. While he taught her the spontaneity that came with "action painting," she showed him how to focus that freedom into a disciplined and potent composition. In the following decade, Krasner finally began to receive recognition from the New York art world as an artist in her own right.

In 1955, Krasner had a break-through exhibition when the Stable Gallery showed a series of collage paintings that contained the destroyed and revised remnants of earlier works. However, as her career began to rise, Pollock's started to decline, and he began drinking heavily. In 1956, when Krasner was in Paris, Pollock was killed in a car crash on Long Island. Despite feelings of grief and guilt, Krasner continued to paint, consistently challenging her earlier work and developing in her style. In 1962, a brain aneurysm almost killed her, and she spent the next two years recovering. In 1965, the Whitechapel Gallery in London mounted the first major retrospective of Krasner's work. Nearly a decade later, *Lee Krasner: Large Paintings* was shown at the Whitney. In 1984, a full-scale retrospective of her career opened at the Houston Museum of Fine Arts and traveled to various venues, including MoMA, making Krasner the first woman to have a retrospective there.

* "Lee Krasner Art Quotes," *The Painter's Keys*, http://quote.robertgenn.com/auth_search.php?authid=874 (accessed July 2009).

† Robert G. Edelman, "Krasner's 'Little Image' Paintings," http://www.artnet.de/magazine_de/usa/features/edelman09-15-08.asp (accessed February 2009).

LEE KRASNER (1908-1984), *UNTITLED*, 1948, OIL ON CANVAS, 42 1/8 X 21 1/8 INCHES, SIGNED

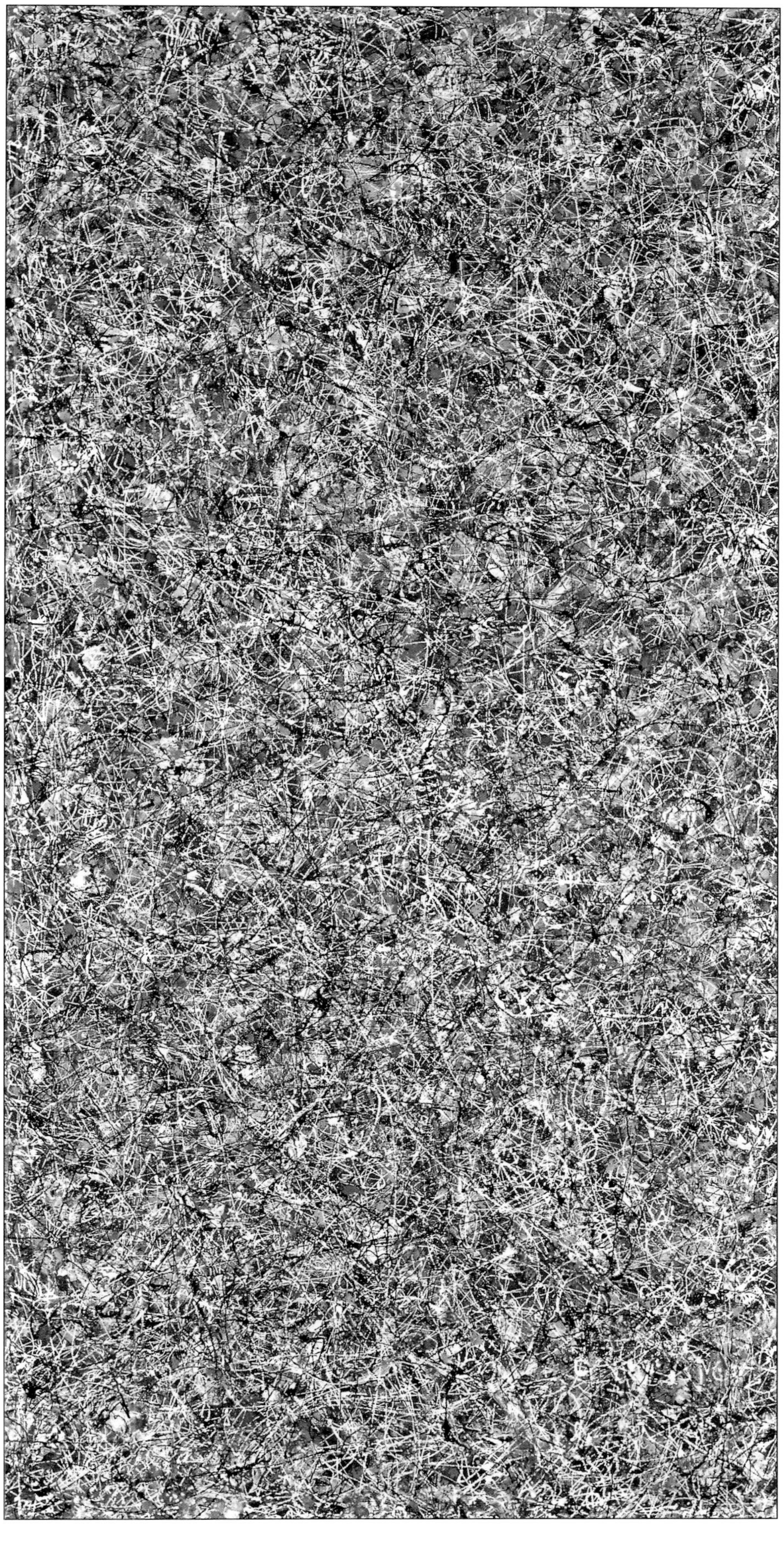

To most people, reality is a confirmation of their expectation. Art can present an alternative to what people think they see or to what they expect to see.*

ALFRED LESLIE

b.1927

Although he may be better known for his larger-than-life-sized, grisaille, figural paintings, **Alfred Leslie** spent the 1950s working in an abstract expressionist vein, creating paintings of explosive color as well as small-scale abstract works on paper. Leslie was born in 1927 to German-Jewish immigrant parents and raised in the Bronx. He developed an early interest in multiple forms of visual art—drawing, sculpting, taking and developing photographs, and shooting film all before the age of fifteen. During World War II, Leslie joined the United States Coast Guard, and in 1947, he used funding from the GI Bill to attend classes at the Art Students League and at New York University where, from 1947 to 1949, he studied with William Baziotes and Tony Smith, among others. In 1949, Clement Greenberg selected Leslie's work for inclusion in his *New Talent* exhibition at the Kootz Gallery. At the same time, MoMA held a screening of Leslie's third film, *Directions: A Walk after the War Games*.

During the 1950s, Leslie's studio became an important meeting place for New York artists, and Leslie was also a regular presence in the world of abstract expressionism, frequenting the Cedar Bar and participating in the 1951 *Ninth Street Show*. His work of the 1950s included collages and paintings—bold rectangles and squares of color that filled the canvas or paper, competing for space, clashing and complementing one another. Leslie met with great success, and his work was shown widely in New York—at MoMA, the Jewish Museum, and the Whitney—and abroad, particularly in Tokyo and Paris. Not content to limit himself to one mode of expression, Leslie continued to make films, including *Pull My Daisy* (1959), which featured Allen Ginsburg and Jack Kerouac. In 1960, he published *The Hasty Papers*, a collection of artwork, poetry, and philosophy with contributions by Ginsberg, Kerouac, and Jean-Paul Sartre, among others. That same year, Leslie's work was included in several major exhibitions including the São Paulo Biennale in Brazil and *Sixty American Painters: Abstract Expressionist Painting of the 1950s* at the Walker Art Center in Minneapolis.

Leslie was and still is considered a master of abstraction; however, in 1962, he changed paths. While most of his contemporaries had begun with figural representation and moved towards abstraction, Leslie's work followed the opposite trajectory. After fifteen years of acclaimed abstract painting, he began creating large-scale nudes and other figural images, often in grisaille or a severely restricted color palette. Unfortunately, a massive studio fire in 1966 destroyed the majority of these works along with many of the master prints of his films. That same year, Frank O'Hara, a poet and good friend of Leslie's, was killed by a Jeep on Fire Island, which prompted Leslie to create *The Killing Cycle* (1967), a collection of five large canvases and numerous studies depicting O'Hara's death.

In the 1970s and 1980s, Leslie's abstract and realist works were included in numerous retrospective and contemporary exhibitions. Although his talent is undisputed in both art forms, the tendency of art history to segregate these two modes of artistic representation has at times adversely affected interpretations of his art. Leslie continues to work, and in 2002, he released a feature-length film about the New York School, *The Cedar Bar*.

* Alfred Leslie quoted by Donald Goddard, "Alfred Leslie: 1951-1962: Expressing the Zeitgeist," http://www.newyorkartworld.com/reviews/leslie2.html (accessed February 2009).

ALFRED LESLIE (B.1927), *HOBOKEN COLLAGE*, 1953-54, COLLAGE AND OIL ON PAPER MOUNTED TO BOARD, 48 X 44 INCHES, SIGNED

ALFRED LESLIE (B.1927), *GREEN SIXTH*, 1959, OIL ON CANVAS, 60 X 66 INCHES

FOR MANY YEARS, I, TOO, STRUGGLED SINGLE-MINDEDLY TO EXPRESS SOCIAL CONFLICT THROUGH MY PAINTING. HOWEVER, GRADUALLY I CAME TO REALIZE THAT CERTAIN THINGS ARE TRUE: THE DEVELOPMENT OF ONE'S AESTHETIC ABILITIES SUFFERS FROM SUCH EMPHASIS; THE CONTENT OF TRULY CREATIVE WORK MUST BE INHERENTLY AESTHETIC OR THE WORK BECOMES MERELY ANOTHER FORM OF ILLUSTRATION; THEREFORE, THE GOAL OF THE ARTIST MUST BE AESTHETIC DEVELOPMENT, AND IN A UNIVERSAL SENSE, TO MAKE IN HIS OWN WAY SOME CONTRIBUTION TO CULTURE.*

Norman Lewis
1909-1979

A native of New York City, **Norman Wilfred Lewis** was the second of three sons born to Bermudan immigrants Diana and Wilfred Lewis. Wilfred was a dock supervisor and longshoreman, and Diana worked as a baker, seamstress, and housekeeper. The Lewis family lived on Lennox Avenue, and for most of Lewis's childhood, they were one of the few black families in Harlem, an experience that made him keenly aware of racism and injustice from an early age. As a teenager, Lewis studied drawing and commercial design at the New York Vocational High School. He held various jobs throughout his schooling—selling newspapers, delivering groceries, pressing and making clothing—but knew he wanted to be an artist from the age of nine. When he was about twenty, Lewis found work on a freighter and spent several years traveling throughout South America and the Caribbean, meeting the people and witnessing the poverty of Bolivia, Uruguay, Jamaica, and elsewhere. Upon his return to the United States, Lewis settled back in New York City.

In the early 1930s, Lewis met Augusta Savage, who ran an arts school in Harlem and was involved with lobbying the Works Progress Administration (WPA) to hire more black artists. From 1933 to 1935, he took classes at the Savage School of Arts and Crafts and attended Columbia University. In 1936, he began working for the Federal Art Project of the WPA, teaching classes at the Harlem Community Arts Center and the George Washington Carver School, where colleagues included Elizabeth Catlett and Charles White. Like many of his fellow WPA artists, Lewis was deeply committed to social and economic equality. He joined the Artists Union and helped to found the Harlem Artists Guild in 1935, which lobbied for and won federal funding for an arts center in Harlem (the Harlem Community Art Center, established in 1937). Lewis also frequented the salons at 306. At this time, his style was grounded in social realism, and his paintings focused on the lives and struggles of urban black Americans. However, in the 1940s, he began to explore abstraction. While he remained active in the struggle for civil rights throughout his life, Lewis was also skeptical about the power of representational art to effect change, explaining in a 1968 interview, "one of the things in my own self education, was the discouraging fact that painting pictures of protest didn't bring about any change."†

In 1945, Lewis's work was included in Alain Locke's exhibition *The Negro Artist Comes of Age,* and the following year, he joined the growing number of New York abstract artists—such as Mark Tobey and David Smith (and later, Charles Seliger)—represented by Marian Willard. From his first solo show at the Willard Gallery in 1949 to the mid-1950s, Lewis's reputation steadily grew, and he developed his own individual style consisting of calligraphic, fluid forms suggesting groups of figures engaged in kinetic activity. A member of the abstract expressionist movement, Lewis befriended artists such as Pollock, Krasner, Kline, de Kooning, and Ad Reinhardt. In 1950, he was the only black artist to participate in the famous closed-door sessions defining abstract expressionism held at Studio 35. A year later, MoMA included his work in *Abstract Painting and Sculpture in America.* Despite a decade of tremendous artistic achievement and consistently favorable reviews, Lewis never received the kind of recognition and financial success his white colleagues enjoyed, and it was only in the late twentieth century that his work began to occupy a central place in histories of American art. Lewis himself was aware of this disparity and of the related expectation in the art world at the time that African American artists document "the black experience."

Throughout his career, Lewis pursued his unique artistic vision while also remaining committed to his political beliefs and dedicated to the people of Harlem. He was a founding member of Spiral (1963), which sought to contribute to the civil rights movement through the visual arts. From 1965 to 1971, he taught for HARYOU-ACT, Inc. (Harlem Youth in Action), an antipoverty program designed to encourage young men and women to stay in school. He joined Benny Andrews, Romare Bearden, Roy DeCarava, Felrath Hines, Raymond Saunders, Alice Neel, and others in picketing the infamous 1969 *Harlem on My Mind* show at the Metropolitan Museum of Art. That same year, along with Bearden and Ernest Crichlow, Lewis co-founded Cinque Gallery, a downtown gallery dedicated to fostering the careers of emerging artists of color. A recipient of a National Endowment for the Arts Grant (1972) and a Guggenheim Memorial Fellowship (1975), Lewis received his first retrospective exhibition in 1976 at the CUNY Graduate Center, New York, just three years before he died.

* Norman Lewis in his 1949 application for a Guggenheim Fellowship printed in Norman Lewis: From the Harlem Renaissance to Abstraction, Kenkeleba Gallery, 1989, p.63.

† Oral history interview with Norman Lewis, 1968 July 14, Archives of American Art, Smithsonian Institution.
  http://www.aaa.si.edu/collections/oralhistories/transcripts/lewis68.htm (accessed February 2009)

NORMAN LEWIS (1909-1979), *REDNECKS,* 1960, OIL ON CANVAS, 51 X 72 INCHES, SIGNED

[PAINTING] IS A CONTINUOUS ATTEMPT AT SOLVING INSOLUBLE PROBLEMS. . . . YOU
JUST KEEP WORKING, AND YOU NEVER GET IT CLEAR TO YOURSELF.*

CONRAD MARCA-RELLI 1913-2000

A member of the first generation of abstract expressionists, **Conrad Marca-Relli** took the epic scale of New York School painting and applied it to collage. Born in Boston in 1913 to Italian immigrant parents, Marca-Relli traveled frequently as a child due to his father's career as a journalist. In 1926, the family settled permanently in New York City, and with his father's encouragement, Marca-Relli began taking night classes at a private art school. In 1930, he briefly attended Cooper Union before setting up a studio in Greenwich Village and working on his own. From 1935 to 1938, Marca-Relli was employed with the Federal Art Project of the WPA, where he met Willem de Kooning, Franz Kline, and John Graham. When the United States entered World War II, Marca-Relli enlisted in the army. After the war, he returned to New York and resumed painting. In 1947, the Niveau Gallery mounted his first solo exhibition, which featured paintings inspired by the haunting dreamscapes of Giorgio de Chirico, whom Marca-Relli met on a trip to Europe the following year. Towards the end of the 1940s, motivated by an exhibition of Arshile Gorky's paintings, Marca-Relli abandoned figural representation for thickly painted abstract forms. In 1949, he became a founding member of the Club, and in 1951, he helped Leo Castelli organize the Ninth Street Show.

From the 1930s to the early 1950s, Marca-Relli had concentrated on painting, but on a 1952 trip to Mexico, he discovered the revolutionary potential of collage, when, in order to adequately capture the texture and tone of the adobe buildings around him, he began cutting strips of canvas and affixing them to his painting. From that point on, Marca-Relli incorporated canvas and raw linen collage elements into his work. He shared with other abstract expressionists a desire to capture intuitive, creative impulses before his rational mind had a chance to repress them. Therefore, Marca-Relli cut his shapes as quickly as possible, in the hopes that speed would bring "free, automatic action, before conscious thought can censor out creativity."[†] He would pin these shapes to supporting canvases, where they became painterly elements, along with the vivid colors he applied through brushwork and spattering. In the 1960s, he began to explore three dimensions more fully by outlining his collaged elements with nail holes. He also incorporated vinyl and cut aluminum to achieve a more industrial style.

Throughout the 1950s, Conrad Marca-Relli continued to work, socialize, and exhibit with the abstract expressionists. His work was shown at the Stable Gallery and the Kootz Gallery, and he also exhibited abroad. In 1953, he bought a house in Springs, East Hampton, near where Krasner and Pollock lived. He also taught at Yale University (1954-1955, 1959-1960) and the University of California at Berkeley (1958). In 1956, when Pollock was killed in a car accident, it was Marca-Relli who identified the body for the police, an experience that prompted him to create *The Death of Jackson Pollock* that year.

After a 1967 retrospective at the Whitney, Marca-Relli spent a decade living and working in Spain before returning to New York in 1980. In 1996, Marca-Relli moved to Parma, Italy, which is where he died in 2000, one year after the Italian government had made him an honorary citizen.

* Michael Kimmelman, "Conrad Marca-Relli, Collagist and Painter, Is Dead at 87," *New York Times,* August 31, 2000.
† Ibid.

CONRAD MARCA-RELLI (1913-2000), *UNTITLED,* 1957, MIXED MEDIA COLLAGE ON CANVAS, 17 3/4 X 23 1/4 INCHES, SIGNED

THE FREEDOM IN MY WORK IS QUITE CONTROLLED. I DON'T CLOSE MY EYES AND
HOPE FOR THE BEST.*

JOAN MITCHELL   1925-1992

An energetic and confident painter, **Joan Mitchell** was born in 1925 and raised in Chicago. Her father, James Herbert Mitchell, was a well-known doctor, and her mother, Marion Strobel Mitchell, was a poet and co-editor of *Poetry* magazine. As a girl, Mitchell was a gifted athlete in tennis—which she played competitively—figure skating, and diving. Her interest in art developed when she was a teenager. Mitchell attended Smith College in 1942, but two years later, she transferred to the Art Institute of Chicago to pursue her passion for painting. From 1943 to 1946, Mitchell spent her summers in Mexico and was particularly influenced by José Clemente Orozco. In 1947, she received both her BFA and an Edward L. Ryerson traveling fellowship from the Institute and spent 1948-1949 in France, working in Paris and Provence. In 1949, Mitchell settled in New York City and became affiliated with the New York School. She frequented the Club and the Cedar Bar, exhibited regularly with the Stable Gallery, and her friends included de Kooning and Kline. In 1951, she participated in the Club's *Ninth Street Show,* and the Whitney selected her work for inclusion in their *Annual of Contemporary Art.* Admired by prominent critics at the time, her work was included in the 1957 *Artists of the New York School: Second Generation,* organized by Meyer Schapiro for the Jewish Museum.

Mitchell abandoned figural art early in her career. By 1951, her style had matured into bold, strokes of color on large canvases. As with other abstract expressionists, her use of gestural brushstrokes and fields of color were not necessarily a negation of the figural or the natural. Although her work was abstract, Mitchell retained a connection to landscapes— natural, industrial, and internal—throughout her career. This link was sometimes evident in titles, such as *Blue Tree, My Landscape II, Cross Section of Bridge,* and *City Landscape.* But usually the connection to landscape was more spatial; as Jane Livingston points out, "she often needed the old-fashioned 'figure-ground' convention for passages to emerge from another space, or the sides and edges of the canvas to support internal activity as though acting like sky around clouds."† While she was clearly working in the realm of abstraction, these compositional traces imported from figural landscape painting set Mitchell on a different path from the first generation of abstract expressionists, who generally favored an all-over pattern of abstraction.‡

In the mid-1950s, Mitchell took up permanent residence in Paris, returning to New York to show her artwork and visit her sister and friends. She was influenced by the analytical modernism of European artists like Cézanne, but Mitchell's painting remained aligned with American abstraction—in her visual style and in her tendency to paint the landscapes of her memory and emotions rather than the external ones she saw on a daily basis. Given the circumstances of her life, these landscapes were often tinted with grief. In the early 1960s, Mitchell's father died; her mother was stricken with cancer and died in 1967. In 1982, after she lost her sister to cancer as well, Mitchell began a series of landscapes based on the childhood stories of a friend in France. Known collectively as the *Grande Vallée* series, these large landscapes convey the combination of exuberance, idealization, and aching loss unique to nostalgia. In 1992, Mitchell herself succumbed to lung cancer, and ten years after her death, the Whitney mounted a major retrospective of her work, which was as widely acclaimed in the twenty-first century as it had been in the middle of the twentieth.

* John Russell, "Joan Mitchell, Abstract Artist, Is Dead at 66," *New York Times,* October 31, 1992.

† Jane Livingston, ed., The Paintings of Joan Mitchell, exh. cat. (University of California Press, 2002), 23. Quoted in Joan Marter, "Review: The Paintings of Joan Mitchell," *Women's Art Journal,* vol. 25, no. 1 (Spring-Summer 2004), 57.

‡ Joan Marter, "Review: The Paintings of Joan Mitchell," 58. In this way, Marter argues, "second generation" becomes a more historical term rather than pejorative.

JOAN MITCHELL (1925-1992), *UNTITLED,* 1953, OIL ON CANVAS, 57 1/2 X 45 INCHES

THE HUMAN BEING IS THE LINK BETWEEN GOD AND THE MATERIAL WORLD. . . .
EVEN A LITTLE WASTE PIECE OF PLASTIC OR A BONE IS JUST AS MUCH ALIVE AS THE
ABSTRACT CONCEPT OF GOD, WHICH IS MEANINGLESS UNLESS IT IS INCARNATED.*

$\mathcal{A}$LFONSO $\mathcal{O}$SSORIO   1916-1990

Alfonso Ossorio was born in 1916 in Manila, the Philippines and was educated in Catholic boarding schools in England before coming to the United States in 1930 to continue his studies at Portsmouth Priory in Providence, Rhode Island. In 1933, he became a U.S. citizen and a year later, matriculated at Harvard University. He received his BA in 1938, after successful completion of a senior thesis entitled *Spiritual Influences on the Visual Image of Christ*. Ossorio began collecting art while he was in college, and in 1936, the Fogg Museum held an exhibition of his collection of works by Thomas Derrick, Eric Gill, Philip Hagreen, David Jones, and Denis Tegetmeier. Also during his time at Harvard, Ossorio created cover illustrations for the 1937 editions of two books of poetry by Arthur Rimbaud. After college, Ossorio studied at the Rhode Island School of Design, and in 1939, the Greek Orthodox Cathedral in Manhattan commissioned him for a work depicting the twelve apostles of Christ. In 1941, Betty Parsons's Wakefield Gallery gave Ossorio his first solo exhibition. In 1943, he enlisted in the U.S. Army and served as a medical illustrator. After his discharge from the army in 1946, he moved to New York City, where he encountered the nascent style of abstract expressionism.

Ossorio's work of the early 1940s was dominated by surrealist still-lifes, landscapes, and portraits executed with haunting detail and an unnerving precision of line. In the late 1940s, he began to explore abstraction, forming vital friendships with Jackson Pollock and Jean Dubuffet, whose work he also collected. Despite their vastly different approaches to painting, Pollock and Dubuffet each showed Ossorio the value of reaching inward for inspiration rather than starting with an object or world external to himself. Ossorio's growing interest in abstraction coincided with his reading Nandor Fodor's *The Search for the Beloved—A Clinical Investigation of the Trauma of Birth and Pre-Natal Conditioning,* which saw human gestation and birth as traumatic, violent processes. In 1950, Ossorio traveled to Victorias, Negros, his first time back in the Philippines since he was ten years old. The return to his homeland opened old wounds from Ossorio's childhood, adolescence, and young adulthood—racial discrimination, conflict about his sexuality, his devoutly Catholic upbringing— and while in Victorias, he produced a stunning set of paintings centered on themes of childhood, birth, sexuality, mythology, and religion. Striking for their hot, vivid, deep colors, their pierced or jagged forms, and their pulsating energy, these works were created using a wax resist technique—Ossorio would apply a light color wash to the paper, draw forms with wax, and then paint in watercolor, which would saturate all areas of the paper except those with wax-drawn shapes.[†] In addition to these works, Ossorio also created a mural for the Chapel of St. Joseph the Worker in Victorias.

After spending much of 1951 in Paris with Dubuffet, Ossorio purchased the East Hampton estate known as the Creeks, which he cultivated into "the Eighth Wonder of the Horticultural World." He also agreed to house the entire collection of the Compagnie de l'Art Brut assembled by Dubuffet at the Creeks, where it stayed until 1962. In the early 1960s, Ossorio began to create his own visionary assemblages, which he labeled "congregations." Within deep wooden frames, Ossorio brought together such disparate found objects as glass eyes, shells, animal bones, shards, pearls, feathers, and driftwood—synthesizing beauty with decay, refinement with crudeness, and reanimating (or resurrecting) these dead objects as vivid art. From the mid-1960s until Ossorio's death in 1990, his work was included in numerous exhibitions in the United States and abroad, including *Documenta III* (Kassel, Germany, 1964); *Contemporary American Sculpture* (Whitney Museum, 1966); *Dada, Surrealism, and their Heritage* (MoMA traveling exhibition, 1968); *30 Years of American Art* (Whitney, 1977); and *Alfonso Ossorio 1940-1980* (Guild Hall Museum, East Hampton, 1980). In 1989, the French art collector Daniel Cordier donated nine Ossorio works to the Centre Pompidou in Paris, and in 1994, the Ossorio Foundation was opened in Southampton. Since 1989, Michael Rosenfeld Gallery has organized ten Alfonso Ossorio exhibitions with the support and assistance of the artist's immediate family and the Ossorio Foundation.

* Alfonso Ossorio interview, 1968 Nov. 19, Archives of American Art, Smithsonian Institution. http://www.aaa.si.edu/collections/oralhistories/transcripts/ossori68.htm (accessed February 2009).

† Francis V. O'Connor, "Alfonso Ossorio's Expressionist Paintings on Paper," *Alfonso Ossorio: The Child Returns, 1950-Philippines*, exh. cat., Michael Rosenfeld Gallery, New York, November 5, 1998 to January 9, 1999, 5-14.

ALFONSO OSSORIO (1916-1990), *FAMILY IN LEAF*, C.1951, OIL AND ENAMEL ON CANVAS, 45 1/2 X 35 INCHES, SIGNED

ALFONSO OSSORIO (1916-1990), *MIRROR POINT*, 1959, OIL AND IMPASTO WITH OBJECTS ON MASONITE, 95 3/4 X 23 3/4 X 2 1/2 INCHES, SIGNED

A WORK OF ART FOR ME IS A WINDOW, A TOUCHSTONE, OR A DOORWAY TO EVERY OTHER HUMAN BEING. . . . IT IS MY CONTACT AND UNION WITH THE UNIVERSE.*

RICHARD POUSETTE-DART 1916-1992

One of the younger members of the New York School painters, **Richard Pousette-Dart** is also credited with having produced the group's first large-scale abstract painting, *Symphony No. 1: The Transcendental,* which he created from 1941 to 1942.[†] This precocious artist, who received little formal training, was born in 1916 in St. Paul, Minnesota and raised in Valhalla, New York by parents who nurtured and supported his interests in the arts. His father, Nathaniel Pousette, was an art critic and artist who believed in the intuitiveness of all creativity. His mother, Flora Louise Dart, was a poet and musician who sought out the relationship between different art forms. His parents combined their names when they got married. Pousette-Dart grew up surrounded by books and his father's art collection, which included works from Africa, the South Pacific, and the Americas. He attended Bard College briefly, but dropped out in 1936 and moved to New York City to become a full-time artist. Although he had no formal training, Pousette-Dart was an assistant to sculptor Paul Manship in the late 1930s. In 1941, he had his first solo exhibition——a group of paintings featuring shapes of color and light encased in black paint——at the Artist's Gallery.

Throughout the 1940s, Pousette-Dart exhibited at the Willard Gallery, the Betty Parsons Gallery, and Peggy Guggenheim's Art of this Century Gallery; he was a member of the Club; and he frequented Studio 35 and the Cedar Bar. In 1951, he was one of the "Irascibles" made famous by Nina Leen's *Life* photograph, and that same year, Pousette-Dart and his wife left New York City for a more contemplative life upstate. Although he lived in Rockland County, Pousette-Dart did not withdraw from the city entirely. He taught art classes at the New School for Social Research, the School of Visual Arts, Columbia University, and the Art Students League. He also exhibited in the city's museums. In 1963, the Whitney organized a mid-career retrospective; in 1969, MoMA organized a traveling exhibition of his work; and in 1973, the Whitney mounted a smaller show of more recent paintings; it was the last major New York exhibition of his work in his lifetime.

Despite Pousette-Dart's considerable talent, the idiosyncratic nature of his paintings contributed to his marginalization. Influenced by surrealism, the psychological studies of Freud and Jung, African art, and Native American art from the Northwest coast, Pousette-Dart pursued the transcendental in art not only in abstract forms, but also in the very way in which he applied paint. In his textured works, thick impasto and solid brushstrokes shimmer with light and color, conveying his belief that "the spiritual doesn't have to do with the lack of the material … if there is a heaven, it is the wonderful working of this world."[‡] While he believed that all art was abstract to some degree, he preferred to call his paintings "presences" and "implosions of color" rather than abstractions. A 1997 survey of his career at the Metropolitan Museum of Art, organized by Lowery Stokes Sims and accompanied by a catalogue, sparked a resurgent scholarly and public interest in his art.

* Michael Klein, "Interior Light: Richard Pousette-Dart," 1997 Features Archives, artnet.com. http://www.artnet.com/magazine_pre2000/features/klein/klein12-10-97.asp (accessed July 2009).

† Hilton Kramer, "Young Pousette-Dart, A Precocious Master, Stood on Frontier," New York Observer, October 5, 2003. http://www.observer.com/node/48148 (accessed February 2009).

‡ Richard Pousette-Dart, personal communication with Jackson Rushing, February 17, 1986. Quoted in Rushing, "Review: Pousette-Dart's Spirit-Object," Art Journal vol. 50, no. 2 (Summer, 1991), 73.

RICHARD POUSETTE-DART (1916-1992), *TWO WOMEN*, 1962. OIL ON CANVAS, 75 × 56 INCHES, SIGNED

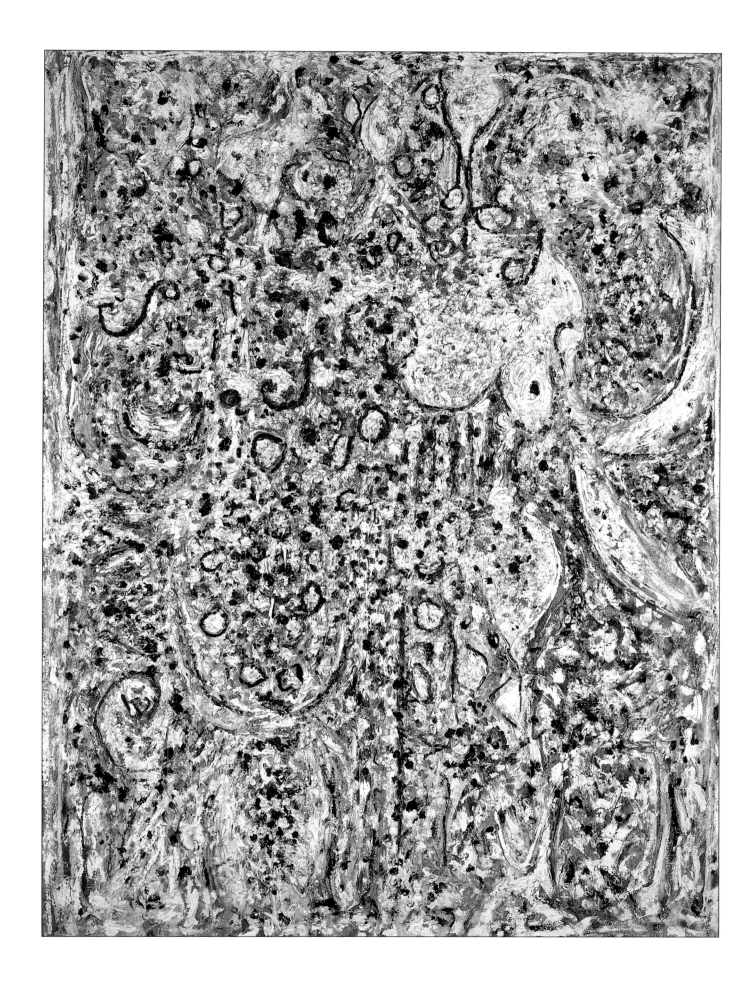

I CAN IMAGINE AN ART THAT WOULD HAVE AN INNOCUOUS SURFACE WHERE YOU DON'T
SEE ANYTHING AT ALL OF INTEREST; YOU WOULDN'T DREAM OF LOOKING AT IT WITH
ANY IDEA THAT IT COULD KNOCK YOU OVER OR HAVE ANY POWER OR ANYTHING, AND
THEN SLOWLY YOU CAN BEGIN TO READ INTO IT ALL KINDS OF WONDERFUL, IMAGINA-
TIVE THINGS THAT YOU CAN SEE IN IT, AND THAT COULD BE A VERY MARVELOUS FORM
OF ART.*

MILTON RESNICK 1917-2004

Born Rachmiel Resnick in 1917, **Milton Resnick** spent his childhood in the Ukraine, where he and his family were threatened by anti-Jewish pogroms during the Russian Civil War. The family fled first to Cuba and then to Brooklyn in 1922. He initially studied architectural drafting and lettering at a trade school, but could not find work when he finished school in the midst of the Depression in 1932. The following year, he enrolled in the fine arts program at the American Artist's School, where he met Ad Reinhardt. In 1937, he met Willem de Kooning, who became a close friend, and in 1938, he joined the WPA. Resnick's artistic pursuits were interrupted in 1940, when he was drafted into the army. When Resnick returned to New York after his discharge in 1945, he resumed painting and began meeting with de Kooning, Kline, Arshile Gorky, and other artists at the Waldorf Cafeteria for discussions about art and abstraction. From 1946 to 1948, Resnick lived in Paris, where he met Constantin Brancusi, Jean Hélion, and Tristan Tzara. He returned to New York, and in 1949, he was one of the founding members of the Club. That same year, Resnick was supposed to have his first solo exhibition, but the dealer cancelled it, causing a major setback to his career. In 1955, the Poindexter Gallery mounted his debut exhibition, but as a result of this six-year delay, Resnick has often been mislabeled a second-generation abstract expressionist.[†]

Resnick was a constant presence on the abstract expressionism scene, despite his ambivalence about being called an abstract expressionist. In 1951, he participated in the Ninth Street Show; his work was exhibited at the Stable Gallery; and in 1957, the Whitney Museum and the Jewish Museum selected his work for inclusion in the 1957 *Annual Exhibition and Artists of the New York School*, respectively. In 1959, he began to increase the scale of his work, creating massive paintings of small, thick gestures that covered the wall-sized canvases, forming a composition of all-over abstraction. Two years later, he started work on his famous *New Bride* (1961-1963), an abstraction of thick white impasto, with flecks of pale color, painted on a nine-by-seventeen-foot canvas. It took Resnick two years to build up the surface of the painting, and this became the first of the impasto monochromes for which he is best known.

Resnick continued to work in an abstract style until the late 1980s, when he started creating a series of gouaches featuring simplified human forms suspended in a field of brushstrokes and color. These isolated, abstracted figures continued in his art of the 1990s. Painted in acrylic and oil in addition to gouache, these figures are often alone, and even when Resnick painted them in pairs, each figure remains isolated, close to but unable to make contact with the other. From 2001 until his death in 2004, Resnick created his "X-Space" paintings, exploring the relationship between color, line, and space from a variety of angles. Regardless of the scale of his paintings or their degree of abstraction, Resnick's gestural brushstrokes and his fascination with the textural and spatial aspects of art remained constant throughout his life.

* Geoffrey Dorfman, "Milton Resnick: In Memoriam," artcritical.com, March 2005 (accessed March 2009).

† David Cohen, "Milton Resnick Was an AbEx Pioneer," *New York Sun*, May 29, 2008. http://www.nysun.com/arts/milton-resnick-was-an-abex-pioneer/78823/ (accessed February 2009).

MILTON RESNICK (1917-2004). *UNTITLED*. 1957. OIL ON PAPER ON BOARD. 26 X 20 INCHES. SIGNED

MILTON RESNICK (1917-2004), *A*, 1957, OIL ON CANVAS, 58 3/16 X 48 9/16 INCHES, SIGNED

I WAS THINKING RECENTLY ABOUT HOW OFTEN SOMEONE WILL ASK ME ABOUT WHAT KIND OF PAINTING I DO ONCE THEY LEARN THAT I AM A PAINTER. I SAY ABSTRACT, HOWEVER IF THEY ASK FURTHER QUESTIONS, I WILL SAY I AM AN ABSTRACT EXPRESSIONIST OR A SURREALIST. BECAUSE I SEEM TO BE SEEN EITHER WAY. HOWEVER I HAVE ALWAYS FELT THAT "ABSTRACT EXPRESSIONISM" WAS WRONGLY NAMED. "ABSTRACT SURREALISM" WOULD HAVE BEEN BETTER. THE BASIS OF ABSTRACT EXPRESSIONISM AND SURREALISM ESPE-CIALLY IN THE 1940S WAS AUTOMATISM WHICH WAS A METHOD EMPLOYED BY BOTH "ABSTRACT EXPRESSIONIST" AND SURREALIST ARTISTS. WHEN I READ THE "LONDON BULLETIN" A SURREALIST MAGA-ZINE PUBLISHED IN ENGLAND, I SAW WORK BY GORDON ONSLOW FORD, ESTEBAN FRANCES, AND WOLFGANG PAALEN AND ONE COULD SEE THE CHANGES THAT INDICATED THAT ABSTRACTION WAS BECOMING MORE RELIANT ON THE USE OF AUTOMATISM—THE IMAGERY WAS TURNING MORE ORGANIC AND LESS AND LESS NAR-RATIVE. HOWARD PUTZEL RECOGNIZED THE CHANGE AND CHALLENGED THE CRITICS TO GIVE THE NEW DIREC-TION A NAME IN HIS 1945 EXHIBITION "A PROBLEM FOR THE CRITICS" AND THE "NEW YORKER MAGAZINE" ART CRITIC BOB COATES WAS THE ONE TO NAME THE FIRST GENERATION, OF WHICH I WAS ONE, "ABSTRACT EXPRESSIONISTS".

CHARLES SELIGER   b.1926

Born in New York in 1926 and raised in Jersey City, **Charles Seliger** has passionately pursued an inner world of organic abstraction, celebrating the structural complexities of natural forms. Seliger spent his teenage years making frequent trips across the Hudson to Manhattan's many museum and gallery exhibitions. Although he never completed high school or received formal art training, Seliger immersed himself in the history of art and experimented with different painting styles including pointillism and cubism. Like many artists of his generation, Seliger was deeply influenced by the surrealists' use of automatism, and throughout his career, he has cultivat-ed an eloquent and poetic style of abstraction that explores the dynamics of order and chaos animating the celestial, geographical, and biological realms. In 1943, he befriended Jimmy Ernst and was quickly drawn into the circle of avant-garde artists championed by Howard Putzel and Peggy Guggenheim. Two years later, at the age of nineteen, Seliger was included in Putzel's groundbreaking exhibi-tion *A Problem for Critics* at 67 Gallery, and he also had his first solo show at Guggenheim's Art of This Century Gallery. Seliger was the youngest artist exhibiting alongside members of the abstract expressionist movement, and he was only twenty years old when MoMA acquired his painting *Natural History: Form within Rock* (1946) for their permanent collection. In 1950, Seliger obtained representation from Marian Willard. While exhibiting at the Willard Gallery, he formed close friendships with several of her other artists, including Mark Tobey, Lyonel Feininger, and Norman Lewis.

In 1949, Seliger had his first solo museum exhibition at the de Young Memorial Museum, San Francisco, and since then, he has had over forty-five solo exhibitions at prominent galleries in New York and abroad. Attracted to the internal structures of plants, insects, and other natural objects and inspired by a wide range of literature in natural history, biology, and physics, Seliger pays homage to nature's infi-nite variety in his abstractions. His paintings have been described as "microscopic views of the natural world," but his abstractions do not directly imitate nature so much as suggest its intrinsic structures.

In 1986, Seliger was given his first retrospective exhibition, at the Solomon R. Guggenheim Museum, which now holds the largest col-lection of his work. In 2003, he received the Pollock-Krasner Foundation's Lee Krasner Award in recognition of his long and illustrious career. Two years later, the Morgan Library and Museum acquired his journals—148 hand-written volumes produced between 1952 and the present. Today, Seliger is best known for his meticulously detailed, small-scale abstractions as well as the techniques he invent-ed and uses to cover the surfaces of his Masonite panels—building up layers of acrylic paint, often sanding or scraping each layer to create texture, and then delineating the forms embedded in the layers of pigment with a fine brush or pen. This labor-intensive tech-nique results in ethereal paintings that give expression to aspects of nature hidden from or invisible to the unaided eye. Since 1989, Michael Rosenfeld Gallery has proudly been the exclusive representative of Charles Seliger.

* Charles Seliger, Journal Entry, July 9, 2009.

CHARLES SELIGER (B.1926), *MOON FROSTY NIGHT*, 1958, OIL ON CANVAS, 27 X 14 INCHES, SIGNED

CHARLES SELIGER (B.1926), *CIRCEAN NIGHT*, 1961, OIL ON CANVAS, 14 X 10 INCHES, SIGNED

RHYTHMS AND COLOR CREATE THE INTERPLAY OF SPACES AND THEREBY GIVE TO ME
THE SYMBOLS NEEDED FOR THE EXPLORATION OF THE INTERIOR WORLD.*

THEODOROS STAMOS 1922-1997

The youngest member of the first generation of abstract expressionists, **Theodoros Stamos** was born in Manhattan in 1922 to Greek immigrant parents and grew up on the Lower East Side. Stamos's interest in nature was sparked at a young age, when he would accompany his father on trips to Pelham Bay and Orchard Beach. He began collecting rocks and shells as a child, a habit he retained throughout his life. In 1936, he received a scholarship to the American Artists' School, where he studied sculpture with Simon Kennedy and Joseph Konzal. At the school, Stamos also met Joseph Solman, who was part of "the Ten," a group of politically conscious artists that included Adolph Gottlieb and Mark Rothko. Solman encouraged Stamos to pursue his interest in painting, and in 1939, Stamos left school to strike out on his own. He supported himself by running a framing business on East 18th Street, where clients included Paul Klee, Fernand Leger, and Arshile Gorky.

In 1943, Stamos met Betty Parsons, who gave him his first solo exhibition at the Wakefield Gallery. His work caught the attention of Gorky and Barnett Newman, who saw in his paintings of this era—which used the surrealist technique of automatism to create mystical, biomorphic visions—an interest in myth and abstraction similar to their own. Over the next few years, Stamos's work was shown in various exhibitions, including the 1945 *Annual Exhibition* at the Whitney and *The Ideographic Picture*, curated by Newman in 1947 for Betty Parsons Gallery. In 1948, Stamos traveled to Europe for the first time, where he visited France, Italy, and Greece, including the island of Lefkada, the birthplace of his parents. Upon his return to New York City, Stamos affirmed his commitment to the exploration of abstraction and continued to create works guided by his firm belief that "for the painter there exists a spiritual power, which communicates life and meaning to material forms, and … he must achieve this power before taking part in the elaboration of forms."[†]

In the 1950s, Stamos's paintings were exhibited regularly in New York, in solo exhibitions and alongside the art of his fellow abstract expressionists, many of whom were a decade or two older than him. He was one of the thirteen "Irascibles" to appear in Nina Leen's *Life* photograph; his work was included in MoMA's *Abstract Painting and Sculpture* in America; and in 1958, he was also part of the museum's New American Painting international traveling exhibition. Stamos retained his interest in the natural and the infinite throughout his life, and his paintings often glow with a light that seems to originate from somewhere behind the paint. In the 1980s, this inner light became even more pronounced in his *Infinity Field* series. With titles that reference specific locations—Jerusalem, Torino, and Lefkada—these luminous works of acrylic on paper seem to vibrate with energy, as if a radiance is just about to burst through the pigment.

*   Theodoros Stamos, undated statement, *Theodoros Stamos—Allegories of Nature: Organic Abstractions, 1945-1949*, exh. cat., Michael Rosenfeld Gallery, November 8, 2001-January 12, 2002, 16.

† Theodoros Stamos, "Why Nature in Art," 1954 lecture quoted in Theodoros Stamos, 22.

THEODOROS STAMOS (1922-1997), *LISTENING HILLS*, 1949, OIL ON MASONITE, 24 X 30 INCHES, SIGNED

THE USE OF COLOR IN MY PAINTINGS IS OF PARAMOUNT IMPORTANCE TO ME.
THROUGH COLOR I HAVE SOUGHT TO CONCENTRATE ON BEAUTY AND HAPPINESS,
RATHER THAN ON MAN'S INHUMAN-ITY TO MAN.*

ALMA THOMAS

1891-1978

Known for her large-scale abstract paintings comprised of rhythmic marks of exuberant color, **Alma Thomas** was born in Columbus, Georgia in 1891. Her parents, John Harris and Amelia Canty Thomas, were both teachers, and Alma Thomas and her three younger sisters grew up around the educated adults their parents often entertained, including Booker T. Washington. In 1907, the family moved to Washington, DC, where Thomas attended the Armstrong Manual Training High School, and from 1911 to 1913, the Miner Normal School for teacher training. Thomas finished with a certificate to teach kindergarten and took a job in Delaware. She returned to DC in 1921, when she enrolled in Howard University as a home economics major, with the intent of becoming a costume designer. When James Herring founded the art department in 1922, Thomas became the first student to major in art; two years later, she was also the first to graduate with a BS in fine arts. From 1930 to 1934, Thomas took summer classes at Columbia University Teachers College, earning her master's in art education. Throughout the 1930s, she continued to work in education and organize community art programs such as the Marionette Club, the School Arts League, and the Junior High School Arts Club. In 1943, when Herring and Alonzo Aden founded the Barnett Aden Gallery—the first gallery in Washington, DC to show work by artists of all races—Thomas became its vice president. She also kept active as a painter, joining the Little Paris Studio, an artists group that included Lois Mailou Jones and Céline Tabary.

In the 1950s, Thomas started to develop the method and style that would make her one of the most innovative American painters of the twentieth century. She embarked on a decade-long formal study of art at American University with painter Jacob Kainen. Departing from realism, Thomas's brushwork loosened, and by the late 1950s, she found her voice in abstraction, patterning geometric shapes in rich colors against solid backgrounds. In 1960, Thomas retired from teaching to devote her time exclusively to art. Although she had been included in various group shows throughout the 1950s, her first solo exhibition, held at the Dupont Theatre Art Gallery, was not until 1960. In 1963, her work was shown in New York for the first time, at the Martha Jackson Gallery's *Artists for CORE* exhibition. In 1972, Thomas was given two major solo exhibitions—*Alma Thomas* at the Whitney Museum and *Alma W. Thomas: A Retrospective* at the Corcoran Gallery in Washington, DC That same year, the mayor of DC, Walter Washington, declared September 9 to be Alma Thomas Day, and in celebration, local TV and radio stations aired programs about her life and work.

The monumental canvases Thomas created in the 1960s and 1970s were informed by the local abstract movement in Washington, DC known as the Washington Color School, which included Morris Louis, Sam Gilliam, and Kenneth Noland, but her interest in color experimentation aligned her more closely to Josef Albers, Johannes Itten, and Wassily Kandinsky. Inspired by nature, and knowledge of recent discoveries in the sciences, and her own observations of earthly and celestial phenomena, Thomas's work was devoid of overt political content. Her dedication to abstraction reflected her belief that modern art at its best could transcend political and historical concerns. However, her prefrence for abstract, joyously expressionistic, gestural strokes of vibrant color was not accompanied by a retreat from historical and social realities. Although the level of Thomas's success as an artist in the 1960s and 1970s meant that she could devote herself exclusively to painting, she never ceased to be a vital force in her community. In addition to her involvement with Artists for CORE (Congress of Racial Equality), Thomas continued to organize art programs and teach art classes to local youth. In 1975, Howard University honored her with its Alumni of Achievement Award, a recognition of her importance to the history of art as well as to the local African American communities touched by her considerable talent as an artist and a teacher.

* H.E. Mahal, "Interviews: Four Afro-American Artists—Approaches to Inhumanity." *Art Gallery* 13, no. 7 (April 1970), 36. Quoted in *Alma Thomas: A Retrospective of the Paintings*, exh. cat., Fort Wayne Museum of Art (New York: Pomegranate Press, 1998), 49.

ALMA THOMAS (1891-1978), *RESURRECTION*, 1966, ACRYLIC ON CANVAS, 36 X 36 INCHES, SIGNED

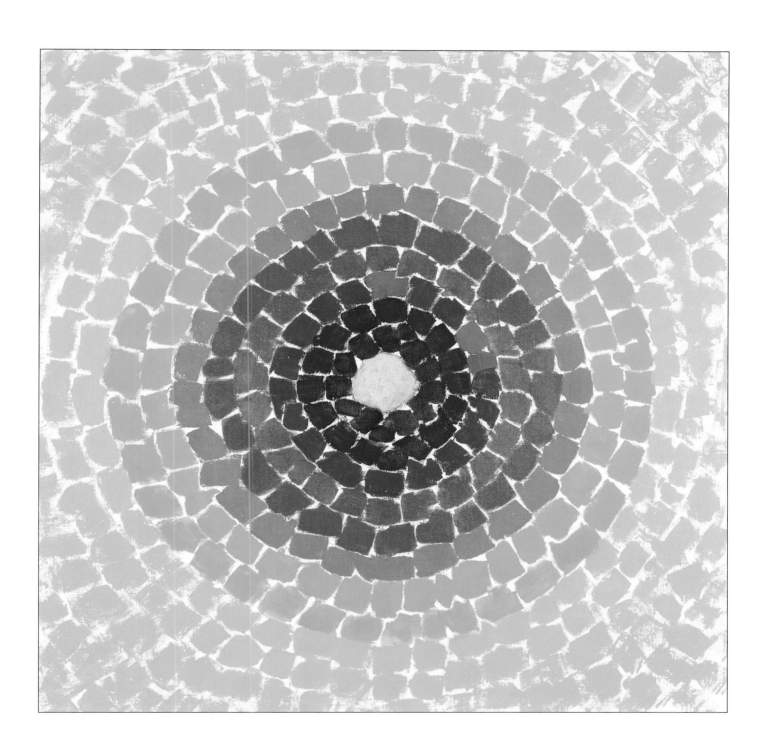

FOR ME, THE ROAD HAS BEEN A ZIG-ZAG INTO AND OUT OF OLD CIVILIZATIONS, SEEKING NEW HORIZONS THROUGH MEDITATION AND CONTEMPLATION. MY SOURCES OF INSPIRATION HAVE GONE FROM THOSE OF MY NATIVE MIDDLE WEST TO THOSE OF MICROSCOPIC WORLDS. I HAVE DISCOVERED MANY A UNIVERSE ON PAVING STONES AND TREE BARKS. I KNOW VERY LITTLE ABOUT WHAT IS GENERALLY CALLED "ABSTRACT" PAINTING. PURE ABSTRACTION WOULD MEAN A TYPE OF PAINTING COMPLETELY UNRELATED TO LIFE, WHICH IS UNACCEPTABLE TO ME. I HAVE SOUGHT TO MAKE MY PAINTING "WHOLE" BUT TO ATTAIN THIS I HAVE USED A WHIRLING MASS. I TAKE UP NO DEFINITE POSITION. MAYBE THIS EXPLAINS SOMEONE'S REMARK WHILE LOOKING AT ONE OF MY PAINTINGS: "WHERE IS THE CENTER?"*

MARK TOBEY 1890-1976

Best known for a visual language inspired by Japanese and Chinese calligraphy, **Mark Tobey** was born in 1890 in Centerville, Wisconsin. In 1909, his family moved to Chicago, and in 1911, Tobey left for New York to become a fashion illustrator. He soon returned to Chicago, and in 1913, he studied at the Art Institute. Back in New York a while later, Tobey had his first solo exhibition at Knoedler & Co. Gallery in 1917. In 1918, he converted to the Baha'i faith. Its teachings, emphasizing the oneness of all religions, all people, and all aspects of the world, had a profound effect on his work. In 1923, Tobey took a job teaching art at the Cornish School and moved to Seattle, where he met and befriended Teng Kuei, a Chinese student at the University of Washington. Through him, Tobey learned about Chinese calligraphic and painting techniques, and his interest developed into an artistic passion. Tobey spent the second half of the 1920s traveling in Europe and the Middle East; he returned in 1929, just in time to be included in Alfred Barr's *Painting and Sculpture by Living Americans* exhibition at MoMA.

In the 1930s, Tobey again left the United States, taking a resident artist position at Darrington Hall in Devonshire, England from 1931 to 1938. During these years, he also traveled extensively in Asia and the Middle East, visiting Colombo, Hong Kong, Shanghai, Palestine, and Japan. He returned to New York in 1938 for what was supposed to be a brief stay, but the impending war in Europe prevented him from leaving the country. After settling back in Seattle, Tobey spent the next several years refining the "white writing" style he had devised while in Devonshire. He also developed his key concepts of "multiple space" and "moving focus." In order to destroy the "hole in the wall" effect of Renaissance perspective (a description offered by Teng Kuei), Tobey conceived of the canvas as a series of spaces, each of which had its own focal point. Together, these multiple spaces formed a compound composition, one unified by calligraphic forms scattered across the canvas. Tobey was thus able to avoid the potential monotony of all-over compositions while also presenting an analysis of space that offered a radical departure from even the shifting planes of cubism and expressionism.[†]

A 1944 show at Willard Gallery brought Tobey national recognition, and his work began to appear in numerous venues. MoMA included him in the 1946 *Fourteen Americans* exhibition; he represented the United States at the 1948 Venice Biennale; the Whitney organized a traveling retrospective of his work in 1951; and that same year, he participated in the São Paulo Biennale. The 1956 American Painting exhibition at the Tate Gallery—which included work by Kline, de Kooning, Motherwell, Pollock, Rothko, and Still—brought Tobey's work back to England, where some of his most important developments had begun.

Not content to simply repeat a successful formula, Tobey turned to Sumi ink as a medium in 1957. He saw the choice of black forms as a logical complement to his previous use of white. In 1960, he participated in *Documenta II* in Kassel, Germany and then settled in Basel, Switzerland, where he stayed for the remainder of his life. Despite his life of constant travel, Tobey's affiliation with the Northwest School helped to establish the region as an important art center in the United States. Through his ties to the Willard Gallery, his work was often viewed alongside and studied in the context of abstract expressionism. Like Richard Pousette-Dart, Tobey's spiritual optimism and physical distance from New York City set him apart from his abstractionist contemporaries, but his interest in the expressive potential of the painted gesture echoed their own artistic concerns.

* Extract from a 1955 letter cited in Arthur L. Dahl, Mark Tobey: Art and Belief (Oxford: George Ronald, 1984), 36. http://www.bahai-library.org/bafa/t/tobey.htm (accessed July 2009).
† William Chapin Seitz, Mark Tobey, exh. cat., Museum of Modern Art (New York), Cleveland Museum of Art, Art Institute of Chicago (1980: Ayer Publishing), 27.

MARK TOBEY (1890-1976), *UNTITLED*, 1957, SUMI INK ON PAPER MOUNTED TO PAPERBOARD, 15 3/4 X 11 1/8 INCHES, SIGNED

My hope is to confront the picture without a ready technique or a pre-pared attitude—a condition which is nevertheless never completely attainable; to have no program and, necessarily then, not preconceived style. To paint no Tworkovs.*

Jack Tworkov

Jack Tworkov was a founding member of the Club (1949). Born in Biala, Poland in 1900, Tworkov emigrated to New York City in 1913, with his mother and younger sister. The family reunited with their father, a tailor, and settled in Manhattan's Lower East Side. Tworkov attended Stuyvesant High School and then went on to Columbia University, majoring in English. Tworkov had planned on becoming a writer, but upon seeing the paintings by Cezanne in an exhibition of French painting at the Brooklyn Museum in 1921, he decided to become an artist. He studied briefly at the National Academy of Design in 1924 and during this time, began spending summers in Provincetown, Massachusetts, where he befriended Karl Knaths and Edwin Dickinson. Tworkov also studied at the Art Students League. After a brief trip to Europe in 1933, Tworkov joined the Federal Art Project of the WPA in 1934, where he got to know Willem de Kooning and Mark Rothko among others. Tworkov's first solo exhibition was held at ACA Gallery in 1940 and although the artist was beginning to experience some success, Tworkov stopped painting in 1942 to help in the war effort as a tool designer. When he resumed painting in 1945, Tworkov found himself increasingly interested in abstraction, which he saw as analogous, rather than antithetical, to figural representation. Tworkov had his first solo museum exhibition at the Baltimore Museum of Art in 1948.

Tworkov's rising prominence as a painter was aided by a 1953 article Fairfield Porter wrote for *ARTNews*. Entitled *Tworkov Paints a Picture,* the piece walked readers through Tworkov's approach to painting and demystified abstraction by presenting it as a deliberate process in which an artist uses color, line, and flame-like brushstroke to express a subject, much like in figural representation. Tworkov's paintings, with their gestural brushstrokes, expressive colors, and balance between control and impulse, were exhibited in numerous shows, including the 1958 *The New American Painting* organized by Museum of Modern Art, which traveled to eight European countries. In 1964, The Whitney Museum of American Art presented a mid-career solo exhibition of the artist's work.

Tworkov was a noted teacher and scholar. From 1963 to 1969 he was Chair of the art department at Yale University. During his tenure, Tworkov took the department in a new direction, opening it up to the exciting transformations taking place on the New York art scene. In 1972, Columbia University awarded Tworkov an honorary Doctor of Humane Letters degree.

By the mid-1960s, Tworkov began to feel that abstract expressionism was losing "the exuberance that was a condition of [its] birth," and the loose brushstrokes and color fields of his earlier style were replaced by his lifelong interest in mathematics and variations on geometric systems. In the 1970s, Tworkov redefined his style again, creating ever more refined themes where rhythmic brushwork played against fields of muted color. In 1982, The Solomon R. Guggenheim presented the last solo exhibition of the artist's work during his lifetime.

* Artist Statement. Stable Gallery catalogue, April 1957.

JACK TWORKOV (1900-1982), *RWB #3*, 1961, OIL ON CANVAS, 64 X 80 INCHES, SIGNED

I THINK ABSTRACTLY BECAUSE I THINK THAT ABSTRACTION IS ANOTHER KIND OF REALITY. AND ALTHOUGH [AS AN ARTIST] YOU MAY SEE A REALISTIC SUBJECT LIKE A GLASS OR TABLE OR CHAIR, YOU HAVE TO . . . TRANSFORM THAT INTO A PICTURE, AND MY WHOLE FEELING IS THAT TO GET THE SPECTATOR INVOLVED, [ART] HAS TO EXTEND HIS VISION, NOT . . . VERIFY THAT WHICH HE ALREADY KNOWS, BUT EXTEND HIS VISION AND HIS WAY OF SEEING SO THAT THERE IS A WIDER EXPERIENCE OPEN . . . TO HIM, AND THIS IS THE WAY I WORK.*

Hale Woodruff

1900-1980

Hale Aspacio Woodruff was born in Cairo, Illinois and raised in Nashville, Tennessee, by his widowed mother. Woodruff's interest in art began when he was a teenager, and after high school, he moved to Indianapolis to study at the John Herron Art Institute. Woodruff's passion for African art was sparked when local art dealer Herman Lieber gave him a book by Carl Einstein entitled Afrikanische Plastik. Although Woodruff spoke no German, he was captivated by the images. Woodruff, who also studied at the Art Institute of Chicago and the Fogg Art Museum of Harvard University, achieved early success as an artist, winning a bronze award in the Harmon Foundation's 1926 competition. Proud of the accomplishments of an Indiana-educated artist, members of the town of Franklin, Indiana raised money for his 1927 trip to Europe. Woodruff stayed in Paris for four years, studying at the Académie Scandinave and the Académie Moderne. While in Paris, he also met Henry Ossawa Tanner, Claude McKay, Augusta Savage, and Walter White of the NAACP. In 1931, when the Depression made it impossible for Woodruff to stay in France any longer, he returned to the United States, taking a teaching position at Atlanta University, where in 1942, he organized the first Atlanta University Annual Exhibition, dedicated to the work of black artists. Throughout the Depression, Atlanta was his home, and Woodruff consistently turned to the Georgia landscape for inspiration. During this time, he was also part of the Federal Art Project.

In 1936, Woodruff spent the summer in Mexico learning mural painting from Diego Rivera. Over the course of his career, Woodruff created several murals in the United States, some with the Project, and some independently. In 1939, the president of Talladega College in Alabama commissioned Woodruff to do a mural commemorating the hundredth anniversary of the Amistad mutiny, and in 1949, he and Charles Alston collaborated on two murals for the Golden State Mutual Life Insurance Company in Los Angeles, depicting the roles African Americans played in the history of California. However, in his eyes, his most significant mural work was his celebrated series of murals entitled Art of the Negro. Commissioned in 1950 for the library of Atlanta University, the works, celebrating the numerous contributions of African Americans to all the arts, were completed in 1951.

Like Romare Bearden and Charles Alston, Woodruff refused to limit himself to either figural representation or abstraction, and he often worked in both visual languages within the same period of his life. Woodruff was well-versed in the principles of European and African abstraction, but his first sustained exposure to abstract expressionism came after 1946, when he took a position as an art professor at New York University. While the work of the New York School had an influence on his art, equally important was his life-long interest in African art. In his abstract paintings of the 1950s and 1960s, expressionistic color and brushwork intersect with patterns, shapes, and pictographic forms inspired by the dynamic compositions of African sculpture, painting, and textile design.

When Spiral was founded in 1963, it was Woodruff who suggested the name, after by the spiral of Archimedes, "because, from a starting point, it moves outward embracing all directions, yet constantly forward."[†] Inspired by the Civil Rights movement, the artists of Spiral, including Bearden, Lewis, Alston, Ernest Crichlow, and Emma Amos, met regularly to discuss the role art would play in the struggle for racial equality. While each member pursued his or her own vision, Spiral lived up to Woodruff's artistic ideals about the relationship between local experience and universal humanity in art. As he explained in an interview, "any black artist who claims that he is creating black art must begin with some black image. The black image can be the environment, it can be the problems that one faces, it can be the look on a man's face. It can be anything. It's got to have this kind of pin-pointed point of departure. But if it's worth its while, it's also got to be universal in its broader impact and its presence."[‡]

* "Hale Woodruff, Painter-Teacher," Obituary, New York Times, September 11, 1980.

† Sharon Patten, African-American Art (New York and London: Oxford University Press, 1998), 185.

‡ Oral history interview with Hale Woodruff, 1968 Nov. 18, Archives of American Art, Smithsonian Institution.

HALE WOODRUFF (1900-1980), SUN, MOON, STAR, C.1970, OIL ON CANVAS, 30 X 25 INCHES, SIGNED

ABSTRACT EXPRESSIONISM

*T*HE 1953 NEW YORK ARTISTS ANNUAL AT THE STABLE GALLERY OFFERS A CHANCE TO SEE WHAT IS GOING ON IN THE STUDIOS, MANY BLOCKS DISTANT FROM 57TH ST., WHERE THE NEWER GENERATION OF PAINTERS AND SCULPTORS INCUBATE WHAT MAY BE—IN SOME INSTANCES—THE LIVELIEST ART OF THE NEAR FUTURE. . . . EXHIBITIONS LIKE THESE SERVE TO BRING ART ALIVE AS A CURRENT ISSUE, AS SOMETHING FLUID AND MOVING, STILL ON THE WAY TO FULFILLMENT AND DECISION, NOT YET PINNED DOWN AND FIXED BY THE VERDICTS OF CRITICS OR MUSEUMS OR "SAFE" COLLECTORS.

— CLEMENT GREENBERG, 1953

Clement Greenberg, "Statement," *New York Artists Annual,* exhibition announcement (New York: Stable Gallery, 1953). Quoted in Irving Sandler, *The New York School: The Painters and Sculptors of the Fifties* (New York: Harper and Row, 1978), 260.

*P*ERHAPS THE HERITAGE FROM THE CUBISTS, IN THE OPINION OF [ABSTRACT EXPRESSIONISTS], HAD DEGENERATED INTO DRY FORMALIST EXERCISES, AND THIS FEELING WHETTED AN APPETITE FOR A RECALL OF EMOTIONAL OVERTONES AND FREE-GESTURE PAINTING. THE NEXT STEP MAY BE IN QUITE AN OPPOSED DIRECTION. IN FACT, SUCH PROTESTS ARE ALREADY HEARD. DOES THIS FLUX AND REFLUX, THIS EVIDENT FICKLENESS OF PURPOSE IN THE ART OF OUR MID-CENTURY PERIOD POINT TO AN UNHEALTHY INSTABILITY, AS WE SO OFTEN HEAR FROM THE UNSYMPATHETIC OBSERVER? ACTUALLY, THIS SO-CALLED "INSTABILITY" IN THE ART OF OUR PERIOD IS ITS HEALTH. IT IS THE SIGN OF LIFE IN IT, A SIGN OF THAT CONSTANT URGE TO REFRESHMENT WHICH, ONLY, WILL KEEP THE LANGUAGE OF ART ALIVE.

— JAMES JOHNSON SWEENEY, 1960

James Johnson Sweeney, "New Directions in Painting," *The Journal of Aesthetics and Art Criticism,* v.18, n.3 (Mar., 1960), 375.

ABSTRACT EXPRESSIONISM

*A*BSTRACT EXPRESSIONISTS WERE ENGAGED IN "TELLING THE TRUTH" AND THEY TALKED A GREAT DEAL ABOUT IT. THIS TRUTH WAS AN EMOTIONAL TRUTH, WHICH WOULD EMERGE FROM THEMSELVES IF THEY KNEW HOW TO ALLOW IT (HERE WAS A STRONG SURREALIST INFLUENCE), AND ONCE TOLD WOULD REVEAL TO THEIR EVENTUAL AUDIENCE . . . . THE PRETENSE OF MANY OF ITS CURRENT EMOTIONAL AND (YES!) SOCIAL ATTITUDES. . . . THE QUALITY OF THIS EXPRES-SIVENESS . . . IS DIFFICULT TO FORMULATE. IT CANNOT FOR ALL THAT BE IGNORED, NOR CAN IT BE RESOLVED BY PURELY FORMAL ANALYSIS. . . . BUT CIR-CUMSPECT AS ONE MUST BE, ONE MUST ALSO RECOGNIZE THAT ART HAS MEAN-ING BEYOND THE PURELY FORMAL RELATION OF ITS INTERNAL PARTS.

— ROBERT GOLDWATER, 1961

Robert Goldwater, "Art and Criticism," Partisan Review, XXVIII, Nos. 5–6 (May–June, 1961), 692. Quoted in Irving Sandler, *The Triumph of American Painting: A History of Abstract Expressionism* (New York: Praeger, 1970), 275.

*F*OR THE EMERGING ABSTRACT EXPRESSIONISTS . . . ART HAD A HIGH INTEL-LECTUAL SERIOUSNESS. IT WAS NO LONGER AN ANTI-MIDDLE-CLASS GAME, AS IT HAD BEEN FOR THE ANTI-ART MASTERS. ART WAS THE GRAIL, AND THE ARTIST, A TORTURED HERO ATTEMPTING THE IMPOSSIBLE TASK OF REACHING IT . . . . MANY OF THE FIRST GENERATION ABSTRACT EXPRESSIONISTS HELD AS A FUNDAMEN-TAL TENET OF THEIR REVOLUTION AGAINST THE PARIS ESTHETIC OF THE 1920S AND 1930S THAT THE WHOLE IDEA OF A VANGUARD IN PAINTING AND ITS COROL-LARIES OF "PROGRESSIVE" MOVEMENTS AND "ISMS," HAD TO BE DISCARDED AS IRRELEVANT. THEY FELT THAT NO STYLES WERE "DEAD," THAT NO APPROACHES WERE INVALID, THAT NOTHING SHOULD BE EXCLUDED FROM ART EXCEPT THE VERY IDEA OF EXCLUSIVITY.

— THOMAS HESS, 1978

Thomas Hess, "Barnett Newman: The Stations of the Cross—Lema Sabachthani," E.A Carmean, Jr. and Eliza A. Rathbone, *American Art at Mid-Century: The Subjects of the Artist,* exh. cat., National Gallery of Art, Washington, DC (1978), 189.

PART TWO: SCULPTURE

SEPTEMBER 10 - OCTOBER 31, 2009

MICHAEL ROSENFELD GALLERY, LLC
NEW YORK, NY

[WITH THE *TOILET* OF 1963] I HAD FINALLY MADE BOB ARNESON. I HAD FINALLY ARRIVED AT A PIECE OF WORK THAT STOOD FIRMLY ON ITS GROUND. IT WAS VULGAR, I WAS VULGAR, I WAS NOT SOPHISTICATED, I WAS A VULGAR PERSON. AND IF YOU'RE NOT SOPHISTICATED, YOU'RE VULGAR. YOU BETTER BE VERY REAL ABOUT THAT. BUT IT WAS ALSO, MORE SIGNIFICANTLY, A VERY IMPORTANT PIECE . . . THE ULTIMATE CERAMIC, AND THAT WAS ALL ABOUT OUR WESTERN CIVILIZATION. IT WAS ALSO ABOUT ALL THE SYMBOLISM AND VERBIAGE THAT ONE WOULD PUT INTO WHAT LATER BECAME POP ART AT THE SAME TIME, NOTIONS AND SUB-NOTIONS, SUBCONSCIOUS AND CONSCIOUS, ABOUT OUR HERITAGE.*

ROBERT ARNESON   1930-1992

Best known for expressionistic, irreverent ceramic self-portraits that doubled as criticisms of humanity's shortcomings, **Robert Arneson** was born in Benicia, California in 1930, to parents who encouraged his interest in art. As a teenager, Arneson was hired to draw cartoons for the *Benicia Herald.* In 1949, he matriculated at Marin Junior College, where he took art courses and continued to draw cartoons and comic strips. Encouraged by his professors, Arneson won a scholarship in his junior year to attend the California College of Arts and Crafts in Oakland, and he received his bachelor's degree in 1954. Afterwards, he stayed in the San Francisco Bay area, completing an MFA from Mills College, where he first encountered the art of Peter Voulkos and was inspired to explore ceramics as a sculptural medium. In 1962, Arneson began a long and distinguished teaching career at University of California Davis, a position he held until a year before his death from liver cancer at age sixty-two.

In 1960, Arneson had his first exhibition: a two-man show with Tony DeLap at the Oakland Art Museum; two years later, his work was included in a crafts exhibition at the DeYoung Museum in San Francisco. In 1963, Arneson was invited to participate in *California Sculpture,* an exhibition of 100 California artists on the roof garden of the Kaiser Center. Daunted by the prospect of representing himself in an exhibition that would include artists he greatly admired, Arneson produced a toilet. Although the work was ultimately pulled from the show, it became the first of several brightly colored ceramic toilets he created. "With *Toilet* . . . Arneson aimed a biting satire at the abstract expressionist aspiration of letting everything within the artist spill out freely in the work. The heavy, monochromatic stoneware of *Toilet* resembled the ceramic sculpture of Voulkos. In addition, Arneson treated the surface with an abstract expressionist touch. Despite his satirical irreverence, Arneson's outrageousness stems from and even pays homage to the iconoclasm of abstract expressionism itself."[†]

In 1974, Arneson met Allan Stone, who became his New York art dealer. That same year, the Museum of Contemporary Art, Chicago and the San Francisco Museum of Art, California mounted a mid-career retrospective of his work. While Arneson's career steadily rose throughout the 1970s, his work was not always well received. In 1981, the Moscone Convention Center rejected a bust of George Moscone, the San Francisco mayor who, with Harvey Milk, was assassinated by Dan White in 1978. The bust was to be the centerpiece of the convention center, but Arneson's choice to include certain elements, such as a Twinkie (signifying White's infamous "Twinkie defense"), was deemed inappropriate. Despite the controversy, Arneson continued to use items from everyday life as a way of creating tension between the ordinary and the traumatic. As Leo Mazow points out, "Arneson exploited the incisive and provocative potential of ubiquitous and seemingly innocuous articles from everyday life."[‡]

Despite Arneson's preference for satire, his provocative and often scathing studies of humanity were always tempered with a deep affection for people. His juxtaposition of opposing elements and sentiments—the comically grotesque with highbrow culture, anger with affection—earned him national acclaim and helped to dislodge the privileged position New York held as the center of the American art world.

* Robert Arneson interviews, 1981 Aug. 14 - 15, Archives of American Art, Smithsonian Institution.

† Jonathan Fineberg, *Art since 1940: Strategies of Being* (Englewood Cliffs, N.J.: Prentice-Hall, Inc, 1995), 286.

‡ Leo Mazow, "Arneson and the Object," *Arneson and the Object,* exh. cat., Palmer Museum of Art (Pennsylvania State University), Greenville County Museum of Art, George Adams Gallery, 2004. http://books.google.com/books?id=d9ovUHhq7kkC&printsec=frontcover&source=gbs_navlinks_s#v=onepage&q=&f=false (accessed July 2009).

ROBERT ARNESON (1930-1992). *UNTITLED.* C.1959. GLAZED CERAMIC. 13 1/2 X 8 1/2 X 8 INCHES. SIGNED

ROBERT ARNESON (1930-1992), *UNTITLED (COILED POT)*, 1961, GLAZED CERAMIC, 25 1/2 X 12 X 12 INCHES

MY MOST PERSISTENTLY RECURRING THOUGHT IS TO WORK IN A SCOPE AS FAR-REACHING AS POSSIBLE; TO EXPRESS A FEELING OF FREEDOM IN ALL ITS NECESSARY RAMIFICATIONS - ITS AWE, BEAUTY, MAGNITUDE, HORROR AND BASENESS. THIS FEELING EMBRACES ANCIENT, PRESENT AND FUTURE WORLDS: FROM CAVES TO JET ENGINES, LANDSCAPES TO OUTER SPACE, FROM VISIBLE NATURE TO THE INNER EYE, ALL ENCOMPASSED IN COHESIVE WORKS OF MY INNER WORLD. THIS TOTAL FREEDOM IS ESSENTIAL.*

ℒEE ℬONTECOU   b.1931

Born in 1931, **Lee Bontecou** grew up in Providence, Rhode Island, where, during World War II, her mother worked in a factory wiring submarine parts. This memory, together with reports she heard about the war and the Holocaust had a profound effect on Bontecou's childhood consciousness. As an adult, she continues to be disturbed by world events, and her work often demonstrates a sharp awareness of the horrors of war and social injustice. Suspicious of the restraints imposed by scholarly and critical attempts to characterize her work, Bontecou has remained independent of any one art movement, but the large-scale wall-mounted sculptures for which she is best known share with abstract expressionist sculpture a drive to challenge the aesthetic and thematic boundaries of art. Bontecou's assemblages are nonspecific and non-narrative, but they nevertheless speak to contemporary politics. Her work has frequently been misinterpreted as a representation/celebration of female sexuality, a characterization that Bontecou rejects, explaining, "As far as the sexual thing goes, it was never an issue…The sexual world is wonderful but it isn't everything."

In 1952, Bontecou attended the Art Students League, where she studied sculpture with William Zorach until 1955. A Fulbright scholarship in 1957 enabled her to spend a year in Italy, where she devised a method of drawing using an acetylene torch. Turning down the torch's oxygen, Bontecou created what she called "worldscapes," soot drawings in which "velvety black forms graduate slowly and atmospherically toward a horizon," foreshadowing, as Mona Hadler points out, "Bontecou's arresting amalgamations of two-and three-dimensional elements."[†] Bontecou returned to New York in 1958 and began working on the large, raw, monochromatic wall-mounted assemblages that have become synonymous with her name. In the 1960s, Bontecou rose to prominence with these abstract wall sculptures, which were constructed from canvas, denim, wire, and welded armatures and often featured a central gaping black hole. In 1960, Leo Castelli gave Bontecou her first solo exhibition, and in 1961, the Whitney Museum of American Art in New York purchased *Untitled* (1961), a large-scale relief fabricated from canvas, rope, and wire, in which the central hole grimaces with "teeth" gleaned from the blade of a band saw. That same year, her work was included in *The Art of Assemblage* at the Museum of Modern Art, New York; she participated in the São Paulo Bienal; and in 1964, she and Louise Bourgeois were the only two women chosen to represent North America in *Documenta III*, Kassel, Germany.

In the 1970s, Bontecou began teaching at Brooklyn College, City University of New York, where she stayed for nearly twenty years. She also created a series of works out of vacuum-formed plastic resembling plants and marine life, which were exhibited at Castelli Gallery but met with limited commercial success. Frustration with the demands of the art market led Bontecou to gradually detach herself from the New York art world, but the often-repeated idea that she became a recluse is misconception. In 2003, a major traveling retrospective of her work was held at the Museum of Contemporary Art, Chicago; the Hammer Museum, Los Angeles; and the Museum of Modern Art, New York. A year later, she received the Skowhegan Medal for Sculpture, and in 2007, Lee Bontecou became a member of the American Academy of Arts and Sciences. Despite a recent heath scare and harassment from white supremacists, Bontecou continues to live and work in rural Pennsylvania.

* Elizabeth A.T. Smith, "Abstract Sinister: Traveling Exhibit of Sculptor Lee Bontecou's Work," *Art in America,* September 1993. http://findarticles.com/p/articles/mi_m1248/is_-n9_v81/ai_14406597/?tag=content;col1 (accessed July 2009)

† Mona Hadler, "Lee Bontecou's 'Warnings,'" *Art Journal,* v. 53, n. 4 (Winter, 1994), 56.

LEE BONTECOU (B.1931). *UNTITLED.* 1963. WELDED STEEL AND PAINT. 21 1/2 X 31 1/4 X 6 1/2 INCHES. SIGNED

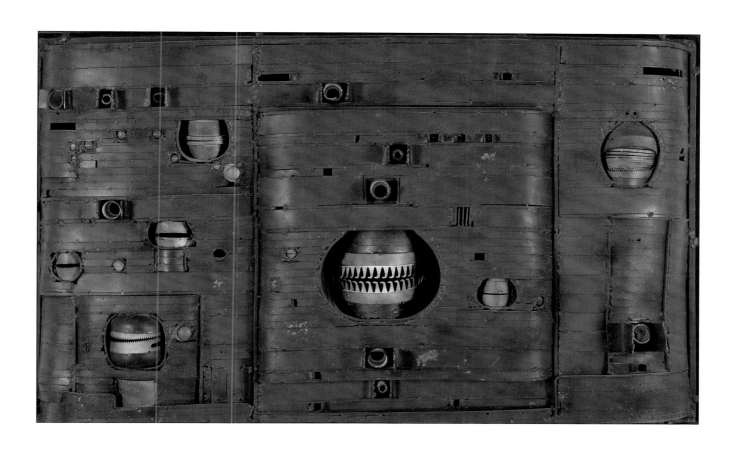

So if you consider art as a privilege, then, by definition, you feel that you do not deserve it. You are continually denying yourself something—denying your sex, denying yourself the tools that an artist needs—because to be a sculptor costs you money. If you consider art a privilege instead of something that society will use, you have to save and suffer for your art, for what you love; you have to deny yourself in the cause of the art. I felt I had to save my husband's money rather than do sculpture that costs money. So the materials I used in the beginning were discarded objects.*

LOUISE BOURGEOIS b.1911

Acknowledged today as a preeminent sculptor of the past half-century, **Louise Bourgeois** was largely ignored before the 1970s when the feminist movement in art brought her sexually charged abstract sculptures in marble, latex, bronze, and wood to wide-scale public attention. Born in 1911 in Paris to tapestry restorationists Louis and Josephine Bourgeois, Louise would often help in the tapestry studio when she was a child, by drawing in sections that needed restoration. She soon became an expert at drawing legs and feet (the parts of the tapestry towards the bottom that most often needed work), and these shapes reappear throughout her body of work. Bourgeois's childhood had a psychological impact on her art as well; her long-suffering mother and charming but chronically unfaithful father produced a household filled with anxiety for the young Bourgeois, which later provided the content for many of her pieces.

In the 1930s Bourgeois attended the Sorbonne, receiving the Baccalauréat in philosophy before studying art history at the Louvre and studio art at the Ecole des Beaux-Arts and the Académie de la Grande Chaumière. Her interest in sculpture sparked when she attended the atelier of Fernand Léger. There, she met surrealists and cubists such as Max Ernst, André Breton, and Marcel Duchamp, all of whom she would later see in New York during World War II. In 1938, Bourgeois opened an art gallery, specializing in works on paper by nineteenth and twentieth century French masters. At this time, she met US art historian Robert Goldwater, and the couple married that same year. Bourgeois moved to New York with Goldwater, took courses at the Art Students League, and began drawing, painting, and making prints. When Bourgeois was pregnant with her third son, in 1941, the family moved to New York's oldest building, the now-demolished Stuyvesant's Folly at 142 East 18th Street. Inspired by the vivid light on the building's roof as well as its placement in the middle of the city but above the chaos of the street, she began using the roof as an open-air studio, creating her *Personages* sculpture series. Tall, lean, rectangular wood sculptures with rounded elements, the works "reflect[ed] not only the forms of the surrounding skyscrapers and therefore the vocabulary of modernism,"[†] but as Bourgeois herself explained, they also "were conceived of and functioned as figures, each given a personality by its shape and articulation, and responding to one another. They were life-size in a real space, and made to be seen in groups."[‡]

In 1945, Bourgeois had her first solo exhibition at the Bertha Schaefer Gallery. That same year, in collaboration with Marcel Duchamp, she curated the exhibition *Documents, France 1940-1944: Art-Literature-Press of the French Underground* for Norlyst Gallery; two years later, Norlyst exhibited her "femmes-maisons"—naked female forms with houses instead of heads and chests. Throughout the 1940s and early 1950s, Bourgeois's painting was included in various group shows such as the Whitney Museum's *Annual of Painting*, but her sculptures did not have their debut exhibition until 1949, at the Peridot Gallery. Despite her early successes and the fact that she was a respected member of the New York School, Bourgeois had only one solo show—her 1964 exhibition at the Stable Gallery—in a period of over twenty years (from 1953 to 1974). During this time, she taught public school in Long Island and art classes at Brooklyn College and the School of Visual Arts. She also traveled extensively and began working in marble and bronze. In 1973, her marble floor piece *Number Seventy-Two (The No March)* was included in the Whitney Biennial. That same year, Bourgeois received a grant from the National Endowment for the Arts, and, unfortunately, her husband also died.

In 1977, Bourgeois was awarded an honorary doctorate of fine arts degree from Yale University; three years later, the National Women's Caucus for Art honored her at its conference in New Orleans; and in 1982, Bourgeois became the first women to have a retrospective at the Museum of Modern Art, New York. In 1993, Bourgeois represented the United States at the Venice Biennale, and the Brooklyn Museum exhibited her first large-scale spider. Over the last twenty years, Bourgeois has received numerous honors and commissions in the United States and her native France. She continues to work today, and her career is remarkable not only for its longevity but also because Bourgeois is a rare kind of artist—one who consistently surprises and delights with startling new work.

* Louise Bourgeois, interview with Donald Kuspit in *Bourgeois* (New York: Vintage Books, Elizabeth Avendon Editions, 1988), .38.

† Josef Helfenstein, *Louise Bourgeois: The Early Work*, exh. cat., Krannert Art Museum, University of Illinois at Urbana-Champaign, May 1-August 2, 2002 (traveling exhibition), 15.

‡ Bourgeois, 1954 published statement, quoted in Helfenstein, 17.

LOUISE BOURGEOIS (B.1911), *UNTITLED*, 1953, BRONZE WITH BLACK PATINA, 51 X 12 X 12 INCHES. EDITION 1/6

I FOUND THAT "ABSTRACT EXPRESSION" IS REALLY THE ONLY [TERM] YOU NEED. BECAUSE IT'S ALL ABSTRACT, IT DOESN'T MATTER IF ITS REALISM, IT'S STILL ABSTRACT, AND IT'S THE GUY'S EXPRESSION. IT DOESN'T MATTER WHO IT IS, THE PERSON'S EXPRESSING HIMSELF. SO IT'S ALL [ART] ABSTRACT EXPRESSION.*

JOHN CHAMBERLAIN

b.1927

Born in 1927 in Rochester Indiana, **John Chamberlain** was raised in Chicago, where he attended the Art Institute from 1951 to 1952, after having served in the US Navy during the Second World War. From 1955 to 1956, Chamberlain attended Black Mountain College near Asheville, North Carolina, where he met poets Charles Olsen, Robert Creely, and Robert Duncan, all of whom taught at the college. Olsen, Creely, and Duncan each had an important influence on Chamberlain; what they did with everyday words, he sought to do with ordinary scraps of metal—arrange the familiar and unspectacular into challenging new configurations that embraced abstraction and defied narrative coherence. In 1956, Chamberlain moved to New York, and the following year, he created *Shortstop*, the first of his sculptures to use the discarded parts of automobiles. In the 1950s, many artists had begun to translate the monumental scale of abstract expressionist painting into sculpture, but Chamberlain added the element of color, using brightly painted scrap metal from the discarded bodies of cars to create voluminous works that exploited sculpture's three-dimensionality. As Lynne Cooke notes, Chamberlain's gestural abstraction and his embrace of the accidental and the spontaneous made his work consistent with abstract expressionism, but to viewers who focused more on his choice of materials "crushed automobile parts in sweet, hard colors redolent of Detroit cars of the 1950s—it was more appropriately aligned with the contemporary work of many Pop [sic] artists."†

Chamberlain had originally turned to scrap metal as a medium out of economic need. Using the discarded metal parts of cabinets, benches, and other objects, he created complex sculptures of interlocking parts that held together almost organically, requiring only spot welding to ensure stability during transport. In the late 1960s, he abandoned scrap metal and began experimenting with other materials: galvanized steel, urethane foam, mineral-coated Plexiglas, and aluminum foil. But in the mid-1970s, he went back to using scrap metal, this time focusing exclusively on car parts. He also established boundaries for himself as a way to stimulate creative thinking; often Chamberlain would limit himself to specific parts (for example, fenders, bumpers, chassis) for a given period of time. In the 1980s, the scale of his work increased dramatically, aided in part by the greater studio space available once he moved to Sarasota, Florida. His work also became more geometric in form, less organic.‡

Chamberlain has continued to develop as an artist throughout his impressive career. He has been honored with numerous exhibitions and awards. In 1961, his work was exhibited at the São Paulo Bienal and in *The Art of Assemblage* at the Museum of Modern Art, New York. In 1964, he was included in the Venice Biennale, and two years later, he received a fellowship from the John Simon Guggenheim Memorial Foundation. By 1971, Chamberlain was established enough for a mid-career retrospective at the Guggenheim Museum, New York. His work was included in the Whitney Biennial in 1973, and in 1977, he won another Guggenheim fellowship. In 1990, he was elected as a member of the American Academy of Arts and Letters; in 1993, the International Sculpture Center in Washington, DC gave him a lifetime achievement award; and in 1997, he was presented with an award from the National Arts Club in New York.

* John Chamberlain Interview by Arne Glimcher, http://www.youtube.com/watch?v=H3zYkrkx-cE (accessed July 2009).

† Lynne Cooke, "John Chamberlain," Dia Center, http://www.diacenter.org/exhibs_b/chamberlain/essay.html (accessed July 2009).

‡ Cooke.

JOHN CHAMBERLAIN (B.1927), *UNTITLED*, 1961, PAINTED METAL, 5 X 4 X 3 1/2 INCHES

IN CONCLUSION, ONE MIGHT SAY THAT ART, LIKE SCIENCE, IS A CONSTANT PROBING OF THE UNKNOWN—A SEEKING. I BELIEVE AN ARTIST SHOULD MAKE ART THAT HE FEELS RELEVANT TO HIS DAY, TAKING INTO ACCOUNT THE WORKS OF ARTISTS OF THE PAST. THE EMPTY SPACES WITHIN AND AROUND A SCULPTURE POSE A CHALLENGE THAT HAS BECOME FOR ME ALMOST AN OBSESSION.*

ℋAROLD ℭOUSINS 1916-1992

Born in Washington, DC in 1916, **Harold Cousins** served in the US Coast Guard during World War II before completing an associate's degree at Howard University in 1947, where he was influenced by the writings of Alain Locke, then head of the Philosophy department. In 1948, he moved to New York City and studied at the Art Students League with William Zorach and Will Barnett. In 1949, with funding from the GI Bill, Cousins left the United States and made his home in Paris, where he studied with the modernist sculptor Ossip Zadkine at L'Académie de la Grande Chaumière.

In Paris, Cousins was captivated by the city's museums; he frequented the Louvre (especially the Egyptian wing) as well as the many ethnographic museums. Among these, his favorite was the Musée de l'homme, where he saw sculpture from Africa, Asia, and the Americas. The mastery of woodworking demonstrated in the African sculptures and masks on display intrigued Cousins, but he was especially inspired by works that combined wood with an array of other materials, which Cousins had already begun to explore in his own work. As he explained, "What especially attracted me was the use of sheaths of metal, often together with nails and chains. These sculptures have a vibrancy that seems to be produced both between the metal elements themselves and between the metal elements and the overall sculptural form."[†]

In the early 1950s, Cousins learned oxyacetylene welding from sculptor Shinkichi Tajiri, and his art developed from figurative forms in terracotta and wood, to works that incorporated more and more metal, and finally, to abstractions of welded steel. He created his first welded steel sculpture in 1952, with scrap metal he bought from junkyards along the Seine, and he had his first major exhibitions of them two years later. In 1957, Cousins coined the term plaiton—a synthesis of the English word "plate" and the French "laiton" (brass)—to describe his sculptures of repeated metal plates welded together in a predetermined order. In discussing these works, Cousins once stated that a key part of the process for him involved "giving special attention to the form of the empty space between the solid elements of a sculpture as well as to the empty space surrounding the sculpture."[‡]

Cousins moved to Brussels, Belgium in 1967, where he worked for the remainder of his life. Throughout his career, he was celebrated in Europe, completing numerous public commissions and exhibiting actively in Brussels and Antwerp as well as various cities in France and Germany. However, it was not until four years after his death that his artwork was shown in his native country, when the Studio Museum in Harlem mounted its 1996 traveling exhibition, *Explorations in the City of Light: African-American Artists in Paris, 1945-65.*

* Harold Cousins, "'Plaiton' Sculpture: Its Origin and Developments," *Leonardo*, v.4 n.4 (Fall 1971), 353.

† Cousins, 351.

‡ Cousins, 351.

HAROLD COUSINS (1916-1992), *PLAITON SUSPENDU (HANGING PLAITON)*, 1958. WELDED STEEL AND BRASS. 59 X 17 X 11 INCHES

HAROLD COUSINS (1916-1992), *LA FORÊT*, C.1960, WELDED BRONZE WITH PATINA ON WOOD BASE, 42 X 47 1/2 X 17 1/2 INCHES

JUST MAKING ART ITSELF IS THE GREAT THING. IT HAS ALWAYS BEEN MY BIGGEST THRILL. IT'S A JOY, A HIGH, BETTER THAN TEN MARTINIS!*

DOROTHY DEHNER 1901-1994

Born in Cleveland, Ohio, **Dorothy Dehner** did not start sculpting until 1955, when she was fifty-four years old. As a teenager, she studied painting with three artistically inclined aunts and dance with a former member of the Denishawn Company, a modern dance troupe and school. By the time she was eighteen, Dehner had lost both of her parents and her only sister. She moved to California to study acting, taking classes at the Pasadena Playhouse and majoring in drama at the University of California, Los Angeles. In the mid-1920s, Dehner moved to New York, where she studied at the Art Students League and met several artists, among them, David Smith. They married in 1927 and lived in Brooklyn.

In 1929, Smith bought an eighteenth century farmhouse at Bolton Landing, in upstate New York, where the couple spent summers before moving there full time in 1940. During their marriage, Dehner drew, painted, and participated in group shows. She also ran their household, assisted Smith with his work, and advised him about his sculptures. In 1948, he translated her drawing *Star Cage* into a sculpture. Although Dehner was passionately pursued art, her career ambitions always took a back seat to those of her husband, who could be demanding and domineering at times. Dehner addressed her conflicted feelings about Bolton Landing and their marriage in two series of drawings: *Life on the Farm,* idyllic representations of everyday life, and *Damnation Series,* featuring "demonic figures surrounded by vultures and bats.... Only years later did she realize how much these drawings expressed the increasing psychological discomfort she felt in the waning years of their marriage."[†]

In 1951, Dehner divorced Smith, left Bolton Landing, and moved back to New York City. She studied painting at Stanley William Hayter's Atelier 17, where she met sculptors Louise Nevelson and David Slivka. In 1953, her work was included in exhibitions at the Museum of Modern Art and the Metropolitan Museum of Art, New York. In 1955, Dehner made her first sculpture. Her earliest sculptures were small, surrealist-influenced bronzes, which she cast using the lost-wax process. According to her, "I was never taught sculpture at all; nobody told me anything. I didn't need it. The minute I had [the wax] in my hands, I knew what to do."[‡] Her work rapidly gained recognition; in 1955, she had a solo exhibition at the Art Institute of Chicago, and in 1957, she joined the prestigious Willard Gallery.

Dehner periodically worked in bronze throughout her career, but in the 1960s, she also began to sculpt in other media, and over the decades, her work grew in scale as well. After the death of her second husband in 1974, Dehner began creating wood sculptures as high as ten feet, and employing a fabricator, she also produced large-scale works in Corten steel. Like the painter Alma Thomas, Dehner found her artistic voice at a later stage in life, and also like Thomas, she more than made up for lost time, earning recognition and awards, and remaining prolific until a pharmacist error rendered her blind shortly before her death. She was a visiting artist at the Tamarind Lithography Workshop in 1970-1971. In 1981, Skidmore College gave her an honorary doctorate, and the following year, she received an award from the Women's Caucus for. She was also the subject of major retrospectives at the Jewish Museum in New York (1965), City University of New York (1991), the Katonah Museum of Art (1993), and the Cleveland Museum of Art (1995).

---

* Dorothy Dehner, quoted in "Dorothy Dehner, 92, Sculptor With a Lyrically Surreal Style" *New York Times* September 23, 1994.
  http://www.nytimes.com/1994/09/23/obituaries/dorothy-dehner-92-sculptor-with-a-lyrically-surreal-style.html?scp=1&sq=dorothy%20dehner&st=cse (accessed July 2009).
† "Dorothy Dehner," op cit.

‡ Elizabeth de Bethune interview with Dorothy Dehner, *Art Journal,* vol.53, no.1 (Spring 1994), 37.

DOROTHY DEHNER (1901-1994), *LONG LANDSCAPE,* 1961, BRONZE WITH PATINA, 47 X 6 X 2 1/2 INCHES

FROM 1950 TO 1963, PARIS WAS THE CENTER OF MY LIFE AND WORK . . . I BEGAN WORKING IN METAL AND DEVELOPED SOME IDEAS FOR JEWELRY. IT WAS A WAY OF TEACHING MYSELF THE CRAFT OF METAL WORK. MY FIRST ATTEMPT AT LARGE-SCALE METAL SCULPTURE WAS IN 1953 WHEN I DID A TWELVE-FOOT-HIGH STEEL ROD SPACE DRAWING, *THE SIGN OF LEDA*. IT CAUGHT THE ATTENTION OF AN IMPORTANT WRITER-COLLECTOR, MICHEL TAPIÉ, WHO COMMISSIONED ME TO BRING IT DOWN TO THREE FEET AND GIVE IT MASS. HE EXPECTED A BRONZE CASTING, BUT I DECIDED THAT I WANTED TO CARRY IT THROUGH A DIRECT TECHNIQUE. THIS PIECE IMPELLED ME TO DISCOVER A WAY OF MAKING MY OWN MATERIAL: A VERY PLASTIC METHOD OF BRAZING STOVE-PIPE IRON WIRE TO FORM THE VOLUMES . . . IT IS NOT A DESIGNER FORM; RATHER, IT IS CREATED MATTER.*

CLAIRE FALKENSTEIN 1908-1997

Born in 1908, in Coos Bay, a small Pacific lumber town in Oregon, **Claire Falkenstein** began sculpting as a child, making small animals out of wet clay at the edge of the bay, where she would often ride her horse at dawn to watch the sun rise over the beach. This daily proximity to seaweed, shells, stones, and driftwood would have a profound effect on her artistic vocabulary as an adult. Her family moved to the San Francisco Bay area, and in 1927, she attended the University of California Berkeley, where she studied art, philosophy, and anthropology and received her AB in 1930. That same year, she had her first solo exhibition at East-West Gallery in San Francisco. Already a radical modernist, Falkenstein received a grant in 1933 to study at Mills College in Oakland, with Alexander Archipenko, who introduced the principles of implied motion and spatial relationships in abstract sculpture. During her studies at Mills, she also met Bauhaus émigrés László Moholy-Nagy and Gyorgy Kepes.

By 1940, Falkenstein, now living in San Francisco, was working predominantly in wood and ceramics, creating abstract, organic three-dimensional forms with moveable parts. Her work was first shown in New York City in 1944, when the Bonestall Gallery mounted a solo exhibition. In the late 1940s, she began teaching at the California School of Fine Arts, where she met Clyfford Still, whose abstract expressionist paintings had an important influence on her approach to sculpture. Influenced by cubism, abstract expressionism, and her interest in negative space and the natural world (which she began to develop as a child on the beach), the work in Falkenstein's 1948 exhibition at the San Francisco Museum of Art demonstrated an evolution to a freer, open-form language.

In 1950, Falkenstein moved to Paris, where she was part of an expatriate community that included Sam Francis, Paul Jenkins, and Mark Tobey. While in Paris, she met artists such as Jean Arp and Alberto Giacometti, as well as the collector and intellectual Michel Tapié. In Europe, Falkenstein developed her mature style, creating some of her most important works, such as the *Sun Series*, sculptures of welded wire that revealed "her rejection of the closed, defined and measurable world of Euclidian geometry in favour [sic] of an active curved space illustrative of her understanding of 'topology.'"† Her work was exhibited extensively, and she and was the only non-German artist included in the 1952 Werkbund exhibition, revived for the first time since its suppression under Hitler.

Falkenstein returned to the United States in 1960, settling in Southern California. Represented by Galerie Stadler in Paris and the Martha Jackson Gallery in New York, she completed numerous public commissions around the world including the gates of the Palazzo Venier dei Leoni in Venice (now in the Peggy Guggenheim Collection, Venice, Italy). Her first public commission in Los Angeles (1963-1965), a welded tube and glass fountain for the California Federal Savings and Loan Association, forced Falkenstein to think in terms of the structure and flow of sculpture, revealing her recurring interest in molecular structure, topology, and cosmology. The most monumental commission of her career was a series of welded doors and glass windows for St. Basil Church in Los Angeles completed in 1969.

* Claire Falkenstein, quoted in *Claire Falkenstein in San Francisco, Paris, Los Angeles, and Now*, exh. cat., Palm Springs Desert Museum, CA, 1980, n.p.

† Wendy Slatkin, "Claire Falkenstein," Delia Gaze, ed., *Dictionary of Women Artists* (Taylor Francis: 1997), 509-511. http://books.google.com/books?id=6_0Y0PALzQMC&dq (accessed July 2009).

CLAIRE FALKENSTEIN (1908-1997), *UNTITLED (SUN)*, 1960, NICKEL PLATED STEEL, 34 X 56 X 13 INCHES

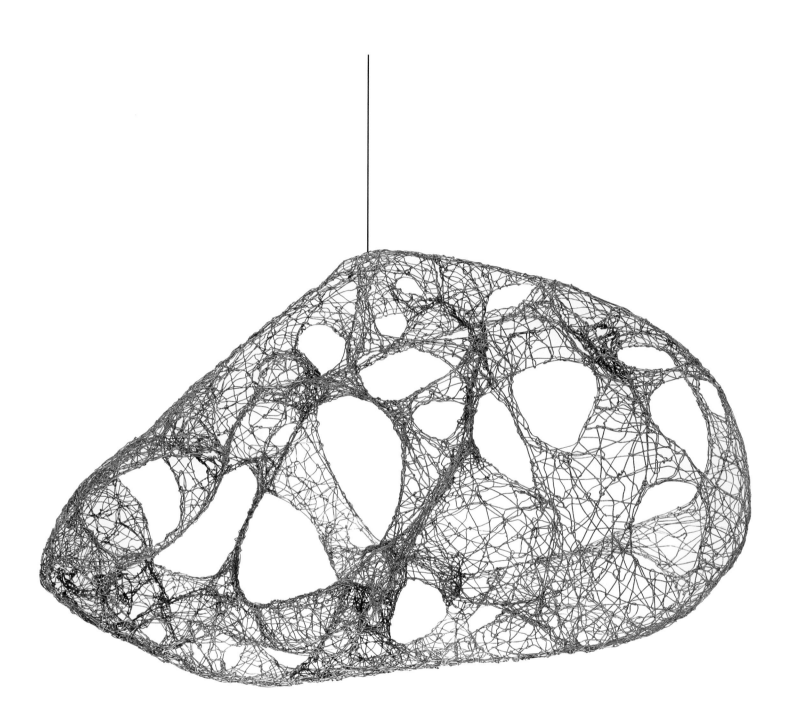

CLAIRE FALKENSTEIN (1908-1997), *UNTITLED (ELEMENT #2)*, C.1965, COPPER AND GLASS, 11 1/2 X 16 X 15 INCHES

I'M NOT AN ABSTRACT EXPRESSIONIST.*

Herbert Ferber 1906-1991

Born in New York in 1906, **Herbert Ferber Silvers** received a Bachelor of Science degree in 1927 and a Doctor of Dental Surgery degree in 1930, both from Columbia University. During his undergraduate studies at Columbia, Ferber became interested in art and art history, which he pursued throughout his time in dental school, taking night classes at the Beaux-Arts Institute of Design and selling etchings he created. After dental school, Ferber received a fellowship to study at the Tiffany Foundation in Oyster Bay, New York. There, he befriended artist David McCosh, with whom he shared a studio on 14th Street. Through McCosh, Ferber met several New York artists, including Theodore Roszak. He joined the Artists Union during the Depression, but unlike many of his peers, he was not involved with the Works Progress Administration (WPA). Instead, Ferber practiced and taught dentistry while working on his sculptures. In the mid-1930s, as he began to search for gallery representation, Ferber dropped the "Silvers" from his name in order to distance himself from the etchings he had made while in dental school. Although he remained a faculty member of the Columbia University School of Dental and Oral Surgery through the 1970s, his change in name marked a change in identity, from a dentist who made art on the side, to an artist who was also a dentist.

During the 1930s, Ferber worked almost exclusively in wood, and although some of his work was consistent with the dominant social realism of the time, he was never fully engaged in this style, in part because of his disillusionment with the direction communism had taken under Josef Stalin. Instead, he became increasingly interested in the work of surrealist artists who were fleeing Europe for the United States. Through the biomorphic forms of surrealism, Ferber "began to see a kind of sculpture which wouldn't easily be made in wood. it would have to have been joined like a piece of furniture in order to get …extensions and thinness."[†] When wood became too limiting, Ferber experimented with lead, which initially allowed him to get the desired degree of thinness but was too soft to survive transport without damage. In 1949, Ferber found his mature style of sculpture—welded metal works that brought together curvilinear and jagged forms in a dynamic tension. With shapes that jutted out in multiple directions, boldly claiming the space around them, these works were truly three-dimensional, illustrating Ferber's belief that space was as integral to sculpture as any medium. His works grew in scale in the 1950s. In 1961, the Whitney Museum of American Art, New York, commissioned *Sculpture as Environment,* a monumental work that opened up the interior space of a sculpture for viewers to inhabit.

Although he objected to being called an abstract expressionist, Ferber was friends with many abstract expressionists, including Mark Rothko, and like many members of the New York School, he was represented by Betty Parsons Gallery. In 1950, he was among the "Irascibles" who protested the juried exhibitions of the Metropolitan Museum of Art, and he became a member of the Club (a.k.a. the Eighth Street Club), founded by abstract expressionists in 1949. But more important than Ferber's social ties to the movement are his stylistic and thematic ones. His work shares several of the innovations of the abstract expressionism, including the magnitude of many of his sculptures and his interest in calligraphic forms. For Ferber, sculpture had the power to capture human gesture and movement—the act behind the stroke of a pen or a brush is rendered in copper or bronze and made mythological through its colossal scale.

* Herbert Ferber interviews, 1968 Apr. 22-1969 Jan. 6, Archives of American Art, Smithsonian Institution. http://www.aaa.si.edu/collections/oralhistories/transcripts/ferber68.htm (accessed February 2009).
† Herbert Ferber interviews, Smithsonian.

HERBERT FERBER (1906-1991), *CALLIGRAPHIC MERCURY II*, 1955, BRAZED BRASS ON WOOD BASE, 50 3/4 X 40 X 16 INCHES, SIGNED

DAVID HARE

1917-1992

A self-taught and acclaimed sculptor, **David Hare** initially made a name for himself as a photographer. Hare was born in New York City in 1917 to parents who supported the arts. His mother, Elizabeth Sage Goodwin, was not only an art collector, but also a backer of the 1913 Armory Show and a friend of prominent twentieth century artists including Constantin Brancusi, Marcel Duchamp, and Walt Kuhn. The family moved to New Mexico in the 1920s, but in the 1930s, Hare returned to the east coast, studying biology and chemistry at Bard College before becoming a professional photographer. Hare settled in Roxbury, Connecticut, where he met Alexander Calder and Arshile Gorky as well as Yves Tanguy, who had married Hare's cousin.

While photography provided Hare an entry into visual culture, he became increasingly interested in other media, particularly sculpture. In the 1940s, Hare developed close relationships with the European surrealists who had fled Nazism for New York. He edited André Breton's surrealist magazine *VVV* from 1941 to 1944, and he also wrote criticism for various literary journals and magazines. In the early 1940s, Hare taught himself to make sculpture, experimenting with materials as diverse as stone, cast bronze, plaster, and wire. His works were soon widely exhibited at such prominent venues as the Samuel Kootz Gallery, the Levy Gallery, and Peggy Guggenheim's famous Art of this Century Gallery. In 1948, he co-founded the Subjects of the Artist School, together with William Baziotes, Robert Motherwell, and Mark Rothko. According to Clyfford Still, the school was intended to be an informal gathering space for artists to think and work. Although the school closed in 1949, it was a precursor for the Eighth Street Club.

Beginning in 1948, Hare spent five years in Paris. He returned to New York in 1953 and began to work with steel rods, initially melting them down and pouring the molten steel into plaster molds, but then eventually also blending steel with alabaster. His work was shown in the São Paulo Bienal of 1951, and in 1958, he was commissioned to create a sculpture for the Uris building (750 Third Avenue) in New York. In the 1950s, Hare's work turned away from the general trajectory of modern American art when he began painting mythological scenes. These works were exhibited to a lukewarm reception at the Guggenheim in 1977. But despite his move away from innovative, dynamic sculptures, Hare nevertheless had a distinguished career. He taught at the Maryland Institute of Art in Baltimore, earning an honorary doctorate from the institution as well. His work continues to circulate internationally, and his sculptures are still considered to be among the best that American modern art has to offer.

* Clement Greenberg quoted in Michael Kimmelman, "David Hare, Sculptor and Photographer, Dies at 75" *New York Times*, December 25, 1992.
  http://www.nytimes.com/1992/12/25/arts/david-hare-sculptor-and-photographer-dies-at-75.html (accessed July 2009).

DAVID HARE (1917-1992), *LEDA'S DREAM OF THE SWAN*, 1960, BRONZE AND STEEL, 59 1/2 X 23 X 19 INCHES

IN SOME WORKS IT IS MY INTENTION TO DEVELOP THE KIND OF FORMS NATURE MIGHT CREATE IF ONLY HEAT AND STEEL WERE AVAILABLE TO HER.*

RICHARD HUNT b.1935

Best known for his open-form welded metal sculptures evocative of insect and plant life, **Richard Howard Hunt** was born in 1935 and raised on Chicago's South Side. Hunt's father was a barber, and his mother worked as a beautician and a librarian. His parents encouraged his considerable artistic talent, enrolling him in classes at the Junior School of the Art Institute of Chicago, which he attended in addition to Englewood High School. After graduation, Hunt continued his studies at the Art Institute's Professional School, pursuing the passion for sculpture he had discovered in high school. In 1953, Hunt encountered the work of welded-metal pioneer Julio González when the Art Institute mounted its *Sculpture of the Twentieth Century* exhibition, and he was inspired to work with metal. By the time he graduated from the Institute, Hunt had basically taught himself how to weld sculptures. In 1957, he received a fellowship to travel to England, France, Italy, and Spain. Hunt returned to the United States, and after a few years in the army, he moved to New York in 1961. In 1962, he won a Guggenheim fellowship; in 1964, he was a visiting artist at Yale—when the art department was under the chairmanship of Jack Tworkov; and in 1971, Hunt became one of the first two black artists to be given a solo show at the Museum of Modern Art in New York. His early-career retrospective, which ran simultaneously with Romare Bearden's MoMA exhibition, featured over fifty works of art and was met with enthusiastic praise from critics.

Hunt stood out from his contemporaries not only through his mastery of welded metal, but also in the distinctive linear gestures that comprised his work. In the 1950s and 1960s, while many modernists were focusing on monolithic forms, Hunt created open-form works of various sizes, whose long and delicate lines combined with slender metal circles or flat metal planes in an effect that critics have characterized as a kind of "drawing in space." In the late 1960s, he added more solid forms, casting metal in addition to welding it. By the 1970s, Hunt was receiving regular commissions to create site-specific sculptures for public locations, and the scale of his work expanded to the colossal. Among the most celebrated of these installations are *I Have Been to the Mountaintop* (1977), the Martin Luther King memorial in Memphis; *Freedmen's Column* (1989) at Howard University; and *Harlem Hybrid* (1976), which was installed on a traffic island on West 125th Street and restored in June of 2008. Although his career has outlasted abstract expressionism by decades, his work shares the convergence of surrealist and expressionist influences visible in the work of many abstract expressionists.

Like Norman Lewis, Hunt chose abstraction at a time when black American artists were expected by the mainstream art world to focus on figural representations of African American history, struggles, and triumphs. And like the paintings of Lewis or the sculptures of Herbert Ferber, Hunt's abstract forms retain their ties to the figural through their emphasis on gesture and movement.

* Richard Hunt quoted in *Richard Hunt*, exh. flier, University of Notre Dame Art Gallery, Notre Dame, Indiana, 1966, n.p.

THE ELEMENTS OF THE PERIODIC SYSTEM IN ALL THEIR COMPOUNDS AND COLORS
BECOME A VAST PALETTE FROM WHICH TO SELECT. . . . ABSTRACT ART, WHICH SEEMS
TO BE FURTHEST REMOVED FROM NATURE, HAS REALLY NEVER LEFT NATURE. WE
LEARN BY OUR DAILY EXPERIENCE OF NATURE'S WAY OF WORKING IN SPACE.*

Ibram Lassaw 1913-2003

Born in Alexandria, Egypt in 1913 to Russian parents, **Ibram Lassaw** discovered his love for sculpture at a young age. When he was a child, his family moved throughout the Mediterranean, and Lassaw lived in Tunis, Malta, Naples, Marseille, and Istanbul before they finally settled in Brooklyn, New York in 1921. In 1926, Lassaw began taking sculpture classes with Dorothea Denslow at the Brooklyn Children's Museum. While he was in high school, he continued his sculpture studies at the Beaux-Arts Institute of Design, where he learned to model from life. Upon finishing high school in 1931, Lassaw took classes at City College, but dropped out after a year. He pursued his interest in the arts full-time, organizing and serving as treasurer for the Unemployed Artists' Association, participating in the Public Works of Art Program, and joining the Federal Arts Project of the WPA, first as a teacher and then as a sculptor. During this time, Lassaw worked on his own sculptures in the various studio spaces he held. In 1933, he made his first abstract sculpture and abandoned figural representation entirely. Lassaw's passion for abstraction led him, in 1937, to organize the American Abstract Artists group, an artists collective focused on promoting abstract art through cooperative exhibitions. In 1942, he enlisted in the army, where he trained as a welder. Although the two years he spent in the army disrupted his work with the AAA, the welding skills he learned would become central to his sculpture a decade later.

In 1949, Lassaw became a member of the Club, and in 1950, he was included in MoMA's *Abstract Painting and Sculpture*. He joined the ranks of artists represented by Kootz Gallery, and the first sale of his sculptures in 1950 enabled Lassaw to buy the equipment necessary for oxyacetylene welding, which he began to use for sculpture in 1951. Like contemporaries Richard Hunt and Herbert Ferber, Lassaw strove to create truly three-dimensional sculpture, and in his work, negative space became a vital part of the overall composition. As with many artists of his generation, including Claire Falkenstein, this interest in the spaces between material forms was influenced by the discovery of atomic energy. But equally important to his work was Lassaw's view of nature, specifically, of the inter-connectedness of all aspects of life. In 1953, he began attending the lectures and reading the books of Buddhist scholar Daisetz Suzuki (who had also influenced the work of Charmion von Wiegand). Lassaw's welded grids in particular evoke the order of natural and celestial systems, as well as Taoism's emphasis on moving through the spaces between things rather than forcing a way through life. As Lassaw's interest in Zen Buddhism and Taoism grew, so did his belief in the intuitiveness of abstraction. As he explained in his 1968 memoir, "Perspectives and Reflections of a Sculptor,""I am not interested in communicating with an audience. To communicate implies that there is something in my mind that I wish to tell someone about. I know in fact that this is not what actually takes place. The work is a 'happening' somewhat independent of my conscious will."†

Lassaw's first retrospective exhibit was organized by the Massachusetts Institute of Technology in 1957. His work was included in the Whitney's 1959 traveling exhibition *Nature in Abstraction,* and that same year, his work was shown at Documenta II in Kassel, Germany. The waning of abstract expressionism did not affect the dynamism and vitality of Lassaw's work. He continued to challenge himself as an artist and sculpture as a medium, sometimes welding, sometimes casting work, and sometimes building a sculpture up from nothing, one drop of melted metal at a time. During his lifetime, his work was regularly shown at galleries and major museums throughout the country. It continues to be an important aspect of American abstraction.

* Ibram Lassaw, "On Inventing Our Own Art," (first published by the American Abstract Artists in 1938). Ibram Lassaw Writings, http://www.ibramlassaw.net/Writings.htm (accessed July 2009).
† Ibram Lassaw, "Perspectives and Reflections of a Sculptor: A Memoir," *Leonardo,* vol. 1 no. 4 (October 1968), 361.

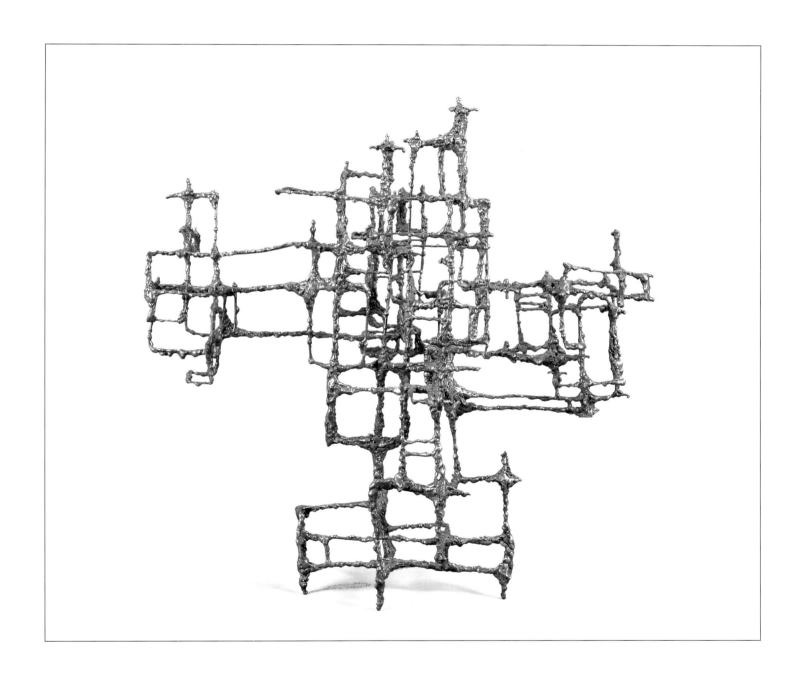

SCULPTURE IS USED BY ME TO EXPRESS THE LIFE OF MAN AS A STRUGGLING INTER-
ACTION BETWEEN HIMSELF AND HIS ENVIRONMENT. SCULPTURE ITSELF IS A PART
OF THIS INTERPLAY.*

SEYMOUR LIPTON   1903-1986

Born in New York City in 1903, **Seymour Lipton** grew up in a Bronx tenement building at a time when much of the borough was still farmland. These rural surroundings enabled Lipton to explore the botanical and animal forms that would later become sources for his work. Lipton's interest in the dialogue between artistic creation and natural phenomena was nurtured by a supportive family and cultivated through numerous visits to New York's Museum of Natural History as well as its many botanical gardens and its zoos. Like Herbert Ferber, Lipton became a dentist, also receiving his degree from Columbia University in 1927. In the late 1920s, he began to explore sculpture, creating clay portraits of family members and friends.

In addition to providing him with financial security, dentistry gave Lipton a foundation in working with metal, a material he would soon use in his artwork. In the early 1930s, he began to devote an increasing amount of time to his art, and while he was friends with artists such as William Baziotes, Adolph Gottlieb, Richard Pousette-Dart, and Will Barnet, Lipton's stern personality inhibited an active social life, a reluctance that often led to his being somewhat alienated from the New York art scene. Although he led a comfortable life, Lipton was also aware of the economic and psychological devastation the Depression had caused New York. In response, he developed a technique of carving directly into wood, creating a richly emotional visual language with which to articulate the desperation of the downtrodden and the unwavering strength of the disenfranchised. In 1935, he exhibited one such early sculpture at the John Reed Club Gallery in New York, and three years later, ACA Gallery mounted Lipton's first solo show, which featured these social-realist-inspired wooden works.

In 1940, Lipton began teaching sculpture at the New School for Social Research, a position he held until 1965. Also at this time, he deviated from wood and started working with brass, lead, and bronze. Choosing these metals for their visual simplicity, which he believed exemplified the universal heroism of the "everyman," Lipton could also now explore various forms of abstraction. Lipton's turn towards increasing abstraction in the 1940s allowed him to fully develop his metaphorical style, which in turn gave him a stronger lexicon for representing the horrors of World War II and questioning the ambiguities of human experience.

In 1950, Lipton arrived at his mature style and began to develop a new technique of brazing on monel metal. Abandoning wood, he began to draw extensively, exploring the automatism that abstract expressionist painters were boasting at the time. Like contemporaries such as Jackson Pollock, Lipton was very much influenced by Carl Jung's work on the unconscious mind and the regenerative forces of nature. He translated these two-dimensional drawings into three-dimensional maquettes that enabled him to revise his ideas before creating the final sculpture. The forms that Lipton produced during this period were often zoomorphic, exemplifying the tension between the souls of nature and the automatism of the machine.

In the years following the 1950s, Lipton's optimism began to rise, and the size of his work grew in proportion. The oxyacetylene torch—invented during the Second World War—allowed him to rework the surfaces of metal sculptures, thus eliminating some of the risks involved with producing large-scale finished works. In 1958, Lipton was awarded a solo exhibition at the Venice Biennale and was thus internationally recognized as part of a small group of highly regarded avant-garde constructivist sculptors. In 1960, he received a prestigious Guggenheim Award, which was followed by several prominent public commissions, including his heroic *Archangel,* currently residing in Lincoln Center's Avery Fischer Hall. Since 2004, Michael Rosenfeld Gallery has been the exclusive representative of the Estate of Seymour Lipton and has presented two solo exhibitions — *Seymour Lipton: Abstract Expressionist Sculptor* (2005) and *Seymour Lipton: Metal* (2008).

* "Seymour Lipton," *Landmarks,* University of Texas Austin, http://landmarks.utexas.edu/artistdetail/Lipton_Seymour (accessed July 2009).

SEYMOUR LIPTON (1903-1986), *INVOCATION #2,* 1949, LEAD AND IRON WITH ARTIST'S WOOD BASE, 87 1/2 X 13 X 13 INCHES

I HAVE ALWAYS HAD MORE IDEAS THAN I COULD EVER EXECUTE IN CLAY, AND THEY CONTINUE TO COME, EVEN TODAY. I REALIZED VERY EARLY IN MY EXPERIENCE WITH CLAY: HERE WAS AN ENDLESS STORY. THE CHALLENGES AND SURPRISES REMAIN CONSTANT.*

b.1927

A pioneering ceramicist affiliated with the Otis Clay Group and a student of Peter Voulkos, **John Mason** was born in 1927, in Madrid, Nebraska. When he was a child, his family moved to Nevada, and the color palette and texture of the Nevada desert had an important impact on his work as an adult. At the age of twenty-two, Mason moved to California. He attended the Los Angeles County Art Institute (now Otis) from 1949 to 1952 and the Chouinard Art Institute from 1953 to 1954. In 1955, he returned to Otis, and met Voulkos, who had been hired while he was away. Voulkos, who ran his classroom like a studio, working alongside his students and allowing them room for individual exploration, had a tremendous influence on Mason, and the two artists became friends. From 1955 to 1957, Mason held a job designing ceramic dinnerware for the Vernon Kilns in LA. During this time, his own work diverged from the scale and functionality of the flatware he designed to support himself. Mason began creating large-scale towers and wall reliefs whose size and texture echoed the monumentality and gestural brushstrokes of abstract expressionist painting.

In the 1960s, Mason began to turn away from the raw expressiveness of these works and towards a smoother, more geometric designs rooted in chiastic and cruciform shapes. Mason's work also increased in size, which led him to question ceramics as an appropriate medium for what he wanted to achieve. The properties of damp clay and the requirement that the works be fired impeded Mason's ideas, and in the early 1970s, he turned to commercially manufactured firebricks as the primary material for his artwork. "Stacked and arranged in geometric formations, these modular units allowed him to create large scale, conceptual sculptures with a precision and speed impossible with traditional ceramic techniques. Moreover, the use of these industrial modules eliminated all traces of personal touch, resulting in anonymous, abstract works whose plans were predicated on elaborating simple ideas of symmetry—translation, rotation, and reflection."[†]

Mason returned to ceramics in the 1980s, creating objects with traces of the functional as well as non-functional sculpture. His interest in geometric abstraction persisted, and Mason began to twist the rigid lines of the geometric, creating a series of vessels entitled *Torque*. This motif of the "large, four sided vessel whose geometric shape was given a distinctive contropposto, axial twist" enabled Mason to delve into questions of formal purity and abstraction. As much as he explores the question of the three-dimensional shape, Mason is also preoccupied with texture and surface. "In his early work, the incredibly tactile surfaces were always balanced by the huge scale of his pieces to create a unified force in space. The surfaces of [later] sculptures glow with an inner light, which only intensifies the dimensional movement of the pieces. The sculptures are fired in earth tones that reflect the source of their medium, yet it still gives them a transcendent aura."[‡]

* http://articles.latimes.com/1997-02-02/entertainment/ca-24536_1_endless-story?pg=2.

† Jeremy Adamson, "John Mason," KPMG Peat Marwick Collection of American Craft: A Gift to the Renwick Gallery (Washington, D.C.: Renwick Gallery, National Museum of American Art, Smithsonian Institution, 1994). http://nmaa-ryder.si.edu/search/artist_bio.cfm?ID=6278 (accessed July 2009).

‡ Kathy Zimmerer, "John Mason," http://artscenecal.com/ArticlesFile/Archive/Articles2000/Articles1100/JMasonA.html (accessed July 2009).

JOHN MASON (B.1927), *UNTITLED*, 1958, GLAZED STONEWARE, 18 1/4 X 7 X 7 INCHES, SIGNED

JOHN MASON (B.1927), *UNTITLED*, 1960, STONEWARE WITH GLAZE, 67 X 30 X 13 INCHES, SIGNED

LIGHT AND SHADE ARE IN THE UNIVERSE, BUT THE CUBE TRANSCENDS AND TRANS-
LATES NATURE INTO A SCULPTURE; THE CUBE GAVE ME THE KEY TO MY STABILITY.*

LOUISE NEVELSON   1907-1977

Born Louise Berliawsky in Kiev, Russia, **Louise Nevelson** emigrated to Rockland, Maine with her family at the age of six. In 1920, she married Charles Nevelson and moved to New York City. In 1924, shortly after the birth of their son, Charles Nevelson moved the family to Mount Vernon, New York. Inspired by an exhibition of Japanese kimonos at the Metropolitan Museum of Art, Nevelson enrolled at the Art Students League in 1929 and studied with Kenneth Hayes Miller and Kimon Nicholaides. She also began to feel constrained by the expectations of a middle class domestic life. In 1931, she left Charles, took her son to relatives in Rockland, and traveled to Munich in order to study with Hans Hofmann, who would become a key figure in the abstract expressionist movement in the United States. After her time in Munich, which was marred by the growing power of the Nazi party, Nevelson departed for Paris before returning home in 1932 and settling in New York.

During the 1930s, Nevelson worked briefly as an assistant for Diego Rivera, and she also taught at the Educational Alliance School of Art under the auspices of the Works Progress Administration (WPA). She began to explore sculpture as a medium, studying with Chaim Gross at the Educational Alliance, and in 1935, her work was included in an exhibition at the Brooklyn Museum. Her first solo show was held in 1941 at the Nierendorf Gallery, and that same year, inspired by Joseph Cornell's poetic collage-boxes and the European surrealists exiled in New York, Nevelson began to incorporate found wooden objects in her assemblages. To Nevelson, wood was immediate, alive, and the only material she could communicate with spontaneously. Her first environment *The Circus, The Clown is the Center of His World* (1943) was shown at the Norlyst Gallery in 1944, and in subsequent years she exhibited actively at Martha Jackson and Pace galleries. Nevelson studied printmaking with Stanley William Hayter at his workshop, Atelier 17, where she met and befriended Dorothy Dehner. A late 1940s trip to Mexico introduced her to Mayan and Aztec art. Influenced by this work as well as African art and folk weavings and fabrics of all kinds, Nevelson broke through to a new kind of work that was entirely her own.

In the 1950s, Nevelson began regularly incorporating discarded and found objects into her work, and her notoriety steadily increased. She became part of the Colette Roberts's Grand Central Moderns Gallery in 1955, where she had regular solo exhibitions, including the 1958 show *Moon Garden + One*, which featured *Sky Cathedral*, the first of her "walls," the large, mounted, wooden reliefs that immediately signify "Nevelson." Shortly after, she joined the stable of artists at the Martha Jackson Gallery, which held its first Nevelson exhibition in 1959. The following year, her work was included in *Sixteen Americans* at the Museum of Modern Art, New York. By 1962, Nevelson had a steady income from her artwork, and the Whitney Museum of American Art had purchased one of her walls, *Young Shadows*.

Nevelson left Martha Jackson Gallery, and in 1963, she established ties with Pace Gallery (now Pace Wildenstein), which continues to exhibit her work regularly. Refusing to become complacent, Nevelson experimented with new sculptural material and approaches, even as she continued to create the black wood walls that established her as a major force in the history of American art. She worked in plastic and metal, and in 1969, she created her first monumental work in Corten steel, an outdoor sculpture commissioned by Princeton University. Later commissions included the 1973 *Sky Covenant* (Corten steel) for Temple Israel in Boston and *Bicentennial Dawn* (1975) for Phildelphia's federal courthouse.

Throughout her career, Nevelson's work was widely exhibited, and she received numerous honors and awards. In 1967, the Whitney mounted her first retrospective exhibition, in 1973, the Walker Art Center in Minneapolis organized a major solo traveling exhibition, and in 1976, she exhibited at the Venice Biennale. Rutgers and Harvard universities both granted her honorary degrees; in 1968, she was elected to the National Institute of Arts and Letters; and in 1971, she received the Brandeis University Creative Arts Award the Skowhegan Medal, both for sculpture.

* "Louise Nevelson's Memorable Quotes," Louise Nevelson Foundation. http://www.louisenevelsonfoundation.org/id19.html (accessed July 2009).

† Louise Nevelson quoted in Brooke Kamin Rapaport, ed., *The Sculpture of Louise Nevelson: Constructing a Legend* (New Haven: Yale University Press, 2007), 27.

LOUISE NEVELSON (1899-1988). *SKY CITY*. 1959. WOOD CONSTRUCTION WITH BLACK PAINT. 47 1/2 X 12 1/2 X 4 INCHES. SIGNED

THE HUMAN BEING IS THE LINK BETWEEN GOD AND THE MATERIAL WORLD. . . .
EVEN A LITTLE WASTE PIECE OF PLASTIC OR A BONE IS JUST AS MUCH ALIVE AS THE
ABSTRACT CONCEPT OF GOD, WHICH IS MEANINGLESS UNLESS IT IS INCARNATED.*

$\mathscr{A}$LFONSO $\mathscr{O}$SSORIO 1916-1990

Alfonso Ossorio was born in 1916 in Manila, the Philippines and was educated in Catholic boarding schools in England before coming to the United States in 1930 to continue his studies at Portsmouth Priory in Providence, Rhode Island. In 1933, he became a U.S. citizen and a year later, matriculated at Harvard University. He received his BA in 1938, after successful completion of a senior thesis entitled *Spiritual Influences on the Visual Image of Christ.* Ossorio began collecting art while he was in college, and in 1936, the Fogg Museum held an exhibition of his collection of works by Thomas Derrick, Eric Gill, Philip Hagreen, David Jones, and Denis Tegetmeier. Also during his time at Harvard, Ossorio created cover illustrations for the 1937 editions of two books of poetry by Arthur Rimbaud. After college, Ossorio studied at the Rhode Island School of Design, and in 1939, the Greek Orthodox Cathedral in Manhattan commissioned him for a work depicting the twelve apostles of Christ. In 1941, Betty Parsons's Wakefield Gallery gave Ossorio his first solo exhibition. In 1943, he enlisted in the U.S. Army and served as a medical illustrator. After his discharge from the army in 1946, he moved to New York City, where he encountered the nascent style of abstract expressionism.

Ossorio's work of the early 1940s was dominated by surrealist still-lifes, landscapes, and portraits executed with haunting detail and an unnerving precision of line. In the late 1940s, he began to explore abstraction, forming vital friendships with Jackson Pollock and Jean Dubuffet, whose work he also collected. Despite their vastly different approaches to painting, Pollock and Dubuffet each showed Ossorio the value of reaching inward for inspiration rather than starting with an object or world external to himself. Ossorio's growing interest in abstraction coincided with his reading Nandor Fodor's *The Search for the Beloved—A Clinical Investigation of the Trauma of Birth and Pre-Natal Conditioning,* which saw human gestation and birth as traumatic, violent processes. In 1950, Ossorio traveled to Victorias, Negros, his first time back in the Philippines since he was ten years old. The return to his homeland opened old wounds from Ossorio's childhood, adolescence, and young adulthood—racial discrimination, conflict about his sexuality, his devoutly Catholic upbringing—and while in Victorias, he produced a stunning set of paintings centered on themes of childhood, birth, sexuality, mythology, and religion. Striking for their hot, vivid, deep colors, their pierced or jagged forms, and their pulsating energy, these works were created using a wax resist technique—Ossorio would apply a light color wash to the paper, draw forms with wax, and then paint in watercolor, which would saturate all areas of the paper except those with wax-drawn shapes.† In addition to these works, Ossorio also created a mural for the Chapel of St. Joseph the Worker in Victorias.

After spending much of 1951 in Paris with Dubuffet, Ossorio purchased the East Hampton estate known as the Creeks, which he cultivated into "the Eighth Wonder of the Horticultural World." He also agreed to house the entire collection of the Compagnie de l'Art Brut assembled by Dubuffet at the Creeks, where it stayed until 1962. In the early 1960s, Ossorio began to create his own visionary assemblages, which he labeled "congregations." Within deep wooden frames, Ossorio brought together such disparate found objects as glass eyes, shells, animal bones, shards, pearls, feathers, and driftwood—synthesizing beauty with decay, refinement with crudeness, and reanimating (or resurrecting) these dead objects as vivid art. From the mid-1960s until Ossorio's death in 1990, his work was included in numerous exhibitions in the United States and abroad, including *Documenta III* (Kassel, Germany, 1964); *Contemporary American Sculpture* (Whitney Museum, 1966); *Dada, Surrealism, and their Heritage* (MoMA traveling exhibition, 1968); *30 Years of American Art* (Whitney, 1977); and *Alfonso Ossorio 1940-1980* (Guild Hall Museum, East Hampton, 1980). In 1989, the French art collector Daniel Cordier donated nine Ossorio works to the Centre Pompidou in Paris, and in 1994, the Ossorio Foundation was opened in Southampton. Since 1989, Michael Rosenfeld Gallery has organized ten Alfonso Ossorio exhibitions with the support and assistance of the artist's immediate family and the Ossorio Foundation.

* Alfonso Ossorio interview, 1968 Nov. 19, Archives of American Art, Smithsonian Institution. http://www.aaa.si.edu/collections/oralhistories/transcripts/ossori68.htm (accessed February 2009).

† Francis V. O'Connor, "Alfonso Ossorio's Expressionist Paintings on Paper," *Alfonso Ossorio: The Child Returns, 1950-Philippines,* exh. cat., Michael Rosenfeld Gallery, New York, November 5, 1998 to January 9, 1999, 5-14.

ALFONSO OSSORIO (1916-1990). *MIRROR BETWEEN.* 1963. CONGREGATION OF MIXED MEDIA. 31 X 28 3/4 X 3 INCHES

THE FORMS THAT I FIND NECESSARY TO ASSERT, ARE MEANT TO BE BLUNT REMINDERS
OF PRIMORDIAL STRIFE AND STRUGGLE, REMINISCENT OF THOSE BRUTE FORCES THAT
NOT ONLY PRODUCE LIFE, BUT IN RETURN THREATENED TO DESTROY IT.*

THEODORE ROSZAK 1907-1981

Born in 1907 in Posen (now Poznan), Poland, **Theodore Roszak** was two years old when his family moved to Chicago, settling amid the city's large Polish community. Roszak's mother encouraged his early interest in art, and in 1920, he entered and won the *Chicago Herald-Examiner's* National Art Contest for Public Schools. He pursued serious art study as a teenager, taking classes at the School of the Art Institute of Chicago. After finishing high school in 1924, Roszak enrolled at the Art Institute full time and won the school's lithograph and Trebilcock awards in his first year. In 1926, he left Chicago briefly for New York, studied privately with George Luks, and took philosophy courses at Columbia University. An Anna Louise Raymond Fellowship in 1929 enabled Roszak to spend two years in Europe, where he saw the haunting paintings of Giorgio de Chirico for the first time. Based in Prague, Roszak also interacted with Czech artists who introduced him to the principles of Bauhaus design and architecture, and he became familiar with the aesthetics and ideology of constructivism.

Roszak returned to the US in 1930, settling in New York. He won a Tiffany Foundation Fellowship in 1931, set up a studio on Staten Island in 1932, and in 1933, the Whitney Museum of American Art included one of his works in their *First Biennial of Contemporary American Painting*. The following year, the Art Institute of Chicago gave him the Eisendrath Award for Painting, and in 1935, Roszak was again represented in the Whitney Biennial with his painting *Fisherman's Bride* (1934), which the museum purchased. That same year, the Roerich Museum's International Art Center (New York) gave Roszak his first solo exhibition. Like many American artists during the Depression, Roszak found regular work through the Federal Art Project of the Works Progress Administration (WPA); he taught at the Design Laboratory, a tuition-free, experimental design school under the aegis of the WPA that promoted Bauhaus and constructivist approaches to art.

During the second half of the 1930s, Roszak had begun working on constructions—sleek, free-standing, and wall-mounted sculptures of plastic and wood rooted in pure geometric abstraction, but constructivist ideology was informed by an optimistic faith in technology, and the destruction wreaked by the machinery of war left Roszak deeply critical of this perspective. In the mid-1940s, he abandoned his constructions, picked up an oxyacetylene torch, and began welding steel sculptures. His interest in welding emerged while he was emoployed at the Brewster Aircraft Corporation in Newark, New Jersey. From 1940 to 1945, he designed and fabricated aircraft, including an experimental bomber. Although Roszak's welded sculptures continued to be abstract, they were expressionistic rather than streamlined, inspired by the organic over the man-made. This shift was presaged in a series of gouaches he did in the early 1940s, which explored questions of myth and ritual. In 1948, the Museum of Modern Art bought its first Roszak sculpture, *Spectre of Kitty Hawk* (1946-1947).

Roszak's career continued to thrive throughout the 1950s and 1960s. In 1956, the Rodin Museum in Paris mounted an exhibition of his work, and *Theodore Roszak*, a traveling mid-career retrospective, was organized by the Walker Art Center, Minneapolis. In 1959, he received a grant from the Ford Foundation, New York and was included in the *Images of Man* exhibition at MoMA. As his career grew, so did the scale of his work and his interest in flight. In the late 1950s, Roszak created an aluminum eagle weighing a full ton with a wingspan of over thirty-five feet for the US Embassy building in London (designed by Eero Saarinen and opened in 1960). For the 1964 World's fair, Roszak welded his colossal *Forms in Transit*—a rocket-shaped, forty-three-foot sculpture comprised of aluminum, steel, and sheet metal—and in 1968, his twenty-five-foot bronze *Sentinel* was installed at the Public Health Laboratories on East 27th Street, New York. Since 2008, Michael Rosenfeld Gallery in cooperation with Jeffrey Hoffeld Fine Art represents the estate of Theodore Roszak.

* Theodore Roszak in Hirschl & Adler Galleries. *Theodore Roszak: Sculpture and Drawings, 1942-1963,* Hirschl & Adler Galleriers, New York, NY 1994.

THEODORE ROSZAK (1907-1981), *STEEL BANNERS*, 1950, WELDED STEEL, 20 1/4 X 15 X 9 1/2 INCHES, SIGNED

THEODORE ROSZAK (1907-1981), *EXPLODING STAR*, 1960-61, PAINTED STEEL, 69 X 107 X 26 1/2 INCHES

I DON'T BELIEVE THE ARTIST HAS ANY PROFESSIONAL DUTY TO THE PUBLIC; THE REVERSE IS THE CASE. IT IS THE ARTIST WHO POSSESSED THE CONCEPT. IT IS THE PUBLIC'S DUTY TO UNDERSTAND . . . . THE ARTIST'S CREATIVE VISION CANNOT GO SO FAR BEYOND THE REST OF THE WORLD THAT HE IS NOT UNDERSTANDABLE. HE IS LIMITED BY HIS TIME. HE IS DEPENDENT UPON THE PAST, BUT HE IS A CONTRIBUT-ING FACTOR TO THE CHARACTER OF HIS TIME. HIS EFFORT IS TO CONTRIBUTE A UNITY THAT HAS NOT EXISTED BEFORE.*

 **DAVID SMITH** 1906-1965

Celebrated for his immense sculptures of welded steel, **David Smith,** born in Decatur, Indiana in 1906, was interested in art from the time he was a teenager, when he enrolled in a correspondence course in cartooning. As a senior in high school, he illustrated the school yearbook, and in 1924, he attended Ohio University Athens for a year, leaving because he was dissatisfied with the quality of art instruc-tion there. After brief periods of time at Notre Dame University in South Bend, Indiana and George Washington University in Washington, DC, Smith moved to New York City, where he found an apartment near Columbia University, in the same building as Dorothy Dehner. In 1927, he and Dehner married and moved to Brooklyn.

In 1929, Smith purchased the farmhouse at Bolton Landing, New York that would eventually become his home as well as an outdoor exhibition/storage site for his work. He built a studio there, installing a forge and anvil, and he and Dehner would spend summers at the farmhouse. In 1931, Smith created his first sculpture, a male head carved from coral and painted. Although Smith sculpted with various materials, in 1933, he acquired an oxyacetylene torch an began welding. Although this innovative method would dominate sculpture in the 1950s and 1960s, in 1933, it was rarely practiced in the United States. He joined the sculpture division of the Works Progress Administration (WPA) in 1937, and in 1938, had his first solo exhibition—of drawings as well as welded sculptures—at the East River Gallery. None of the works sold, a situation that would hound Smith again later in his career. In addition to welding, Smith created a series of cast bronze medals in response to the chokehold fascism had obtained over much of Europe at the time. Entitled *Medals for Dishonor,* the works in the series call attention to corruption, brutality, and crimes against humanity. In 1941, Smith participated in two important traveling exhibitions organized by the Museum of Modern Art, New York—*Fifteen American Sculptors* and *Twentieth Century Sculptures and Constructions.* He was also included in the *Whitney Annual* at the Whitney Museum of American Art, New York.

Despite his growing success as an artist, Smith could not yet support himself through art alone. In the 1940s, he took a job on the assembly line at American Locomotive Company, putting together locomotives and M7 destroyer tanks. Although the job took Smith away from his artwork, it also gave him valuable welding experience. By the time he quit, he felt a greater mastery of welding, and the late 1940s became a period of tremendous productivity. In 1948, Smith began teaching at Sarah Lawrence College, but two successive fellowships from the John Simon Guggenheim Memorial Foundation, in 1950 and 1951, enabled him to leave teaching and devote his time exclusively to his artwork. During these years, Smith developed a complex and personal symbolic language that he employed in his sculpture.

In the early 1950s, despite the personal setback of his divorce from Dehner, Smith grew as an artist, befriending members of the New York School, developing new approaches to sculpture, and exhibiting at various national and international venues. His work was included in MoMA's 1953 international traveling exhibition *Twelve Modern American Painters and Sculptors,* alongside works by abstract expression-ists Jackson Pollock and Arshile Gorky. In 1956, he began painting the surfaces of his metal sculptures, and the following year, he started to make large scale sculptures of burnished stainless steel, which he designed to interact with the light and colors of their surroundings in ways that gave the works depth and also incorporated an element of chance—the same sculpture would acquire different character-istics in different environments. Thus, while many of his contemporaries were working through ways to use negative space as one of the main components of a sculpture, Smith extended questions of presence and absence to the entire environment around the individual art-work. In 1958, Smith had a solo exhibition at MoMA, and in 1961, the museum organized a second solo show, one that traveled to other venues. That same year, Smith began his *Cubi* series, the last monumental series he completed before his death in 1965.

* Garnett McCoy, ed., *David Smith* (New York: Praeger, 1973), 58. Quoted in Bénédicte Ajac and Nat Trotman, "Chronology," *David Smith: A Centennial,* exh. cat., Solomon R. Guggenheim Museum, New York, February 3–May 14, 2006, 403.

DAVID SMITH (1906-1965). *ALBANY VII,* 1959. PAINTED STEEL. 36 X 17 1/2 X 14 INCHES. SIGNED

EVERYTHING HAS LIFE. IN MY PAST THE NECESSITIES OF OUR LIVING AND THE CON-
DITIONS OF THE SOCIETY OF PEOPLE HAVE SENT ME OUT TO BE ALONE—OUT TO THE
COUNTRY, ON THE SEA. ONE CAN BE AS LONELY AS ONE WISHES, BUT IT IS IMPOS-
SIBLE TO BE ALONE . . . EVEN ON THE SALT AND STERILE SEA, WAIT FOR THE CALM
AND LIE OVER THE LOW RAIL TO STARE DOWN INTO THE BLUE GLASS WATER AND
WHAT AT FIRST SEEMS A PURE MEDIUM BEGINS TO DANCE WITH MOTES, DARTING
SPECKS, AND DOWN AT THE THRESHOLD OF THE DARK, OMINOUS SHADOWS TURN
AND CAREEN ABOUT . . . IT IS UNBEARABLE TO CONCEIVE THAT ANYTHING CANNOT
HAVE LIFE.*

RICHARD STANKIEWICZ 1922-1983

An emerging artist during the peak years of abstract expressionism, **Richard Stankiewicz** brought a sense of humor and lightness to the large, heavy sculptures he constructed from found scraps of metal. Born in Philadelphia in 1922, Stankiewicz lost his father in a railroad accident at the age of two. His mother moved her three children to Detroit, where Stankiewicz grew up in a predominantly German and Polish immigrant community. He attended Cass Technical High School, studying mechanical drafting, volumetric geometry, engineering, art, and music. Despite a scholarship for the Cranbrook Academy of Art, Stankiewicz could not afford college, and in 1941, he joined the US Navy. Discharged in 1947, he eventually made his way to New York City and then to Europe where in 1950, he was able to use funding from the GI Bill to study painting at Atelier Fernand Léger and sculpture with Ossip Zadkine.

In 1952, Stankiewicz became a member of Hansa Gallery, a cooperative gallery founded by former students of Hans Hofmann, including Jan Müller, Jean Follet, and Wolf Kahn. Throughout the 1950s, he supported himself as a freelance draftsman while experimenting with various materials for sculpture. He created a series of insects sculpted from wire that were shown at Hansa in 1953, and that same year, he exhibited his welded steel sculptures which were hailed by Fairfield Porter as evidence that "life is stronger than the machine."[†] A strong supporter of Stankiewicz's work, Porter also wrote an article, "Stankiewicz Makes a Sculpture," for the September 1955 issue of ARTNews. For the remainder of the decade, Stankiewicz's work was increasingly well received, and he participated in numerous group and solo shows, including *Young America 1957* at the Whitney Museum of American Art, *Irons in the Fire* at the Contemporary Arts Museum in Houston (1957), the Venice Biennale (1958), and a one-man exhibition at the Stable Gallery in 1959.

A "masterful composer and animator," Stankiewicz coaxed living forms out of rusted, abandoned, industrial detritus. His sense of whimsy, controlled spontaneity, and the uncanny element of the inanimate becoming animate tie his sculpture to surrealism, but as Emmie Donadio adds, Stankiewicz's work emerges out of early twentieth century modernism and prefigures what would follow in the second half of the century.[‡] This placement on the threshold of early and late twentieth century modernism served Stankiewicz well, as he continued to exhibit and develop his sculpture throughout the 1960s and 1970s, establishing relationships with New York galleries even after he left the city in 1962 for rural Massachusetts.

Although scrap metal had served Stankiewicz well, he continued to grow as an artist, discovering new materials to work with. In 1969, he traveled to Australia, where he produced fifteen steel sculptures in collaboration with the Transfield Foundry in Sydney. Returning to the United States in 1970, he established a relationship with Nash Foundry in Pittsfield, Massachusetts and from that point on worked exclusively in milled steel. In 1975, he exhibited his largest pieces, a 1974 untitled sculpture ten feet high and thirteen feet in width and depth. His final works demonstrate his consistent mining of the monumental, dynamic, multi-dimensional potential of sculpture.

* Richard Stankiewicz, quoted in Emmie Donadio, "Miracle in the Scrap Heap: The Sculpture of Richard Stankiewicz," Miracle in the Scrap Heap: The Sculpture of Richard Stankiewicz, exh. cat., Addison Gallery of American Art, Philips Academy, Andover, Massachusetts, 15.

† Fairfield Porter, ARTNews (December 1953), quoted in Miracle in the Scrap Heap: The Sculpture of Richard Stankiewicz, 150.

‡ Miracle in the Scrap Heap: The Sculpture of Richard Stankiewicz, 12.

RICHARD STANKIEWICZ (1922-1983). *SEATED LADY*. 1954. WELDED SCRAP METAL. 49 X 23 X 17 INCHES

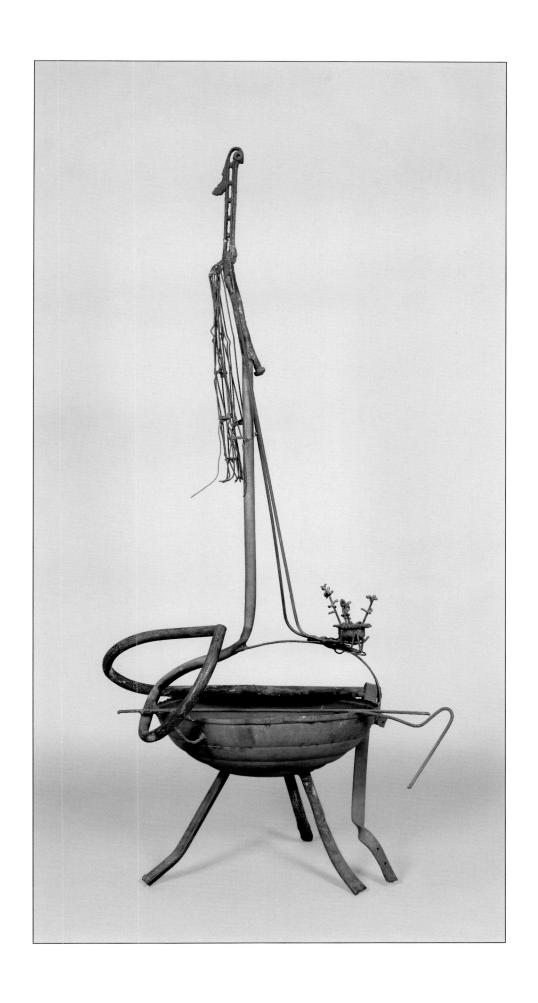

RICHARD STANKIEWICZ (1922-1983), *UNTITLED C (1961-22)*, 1961, WELDED SCRAP METAL, 34 1/2 X 24 X 33 INCHES, SIGNED

IN MY LIFE, I SEE NO DIFFERENCE BETWEEN MAKING POTS, COOKING, AND GROW-
ING VEGETABLES. THEY ARE ALL RELATED. HOWEVER, THERE IS A NEED FOR ME TO
WORK IN CLAY. IT IS SO GRATIFYING, AND I GET SO MUCH JOY FROM IT, AND IT GIVES
ME MANY ANSWERS FOR MY LIFE.*

TOSHIKO TAKAEZU   b.1922

Among the most prominent ceramics artists in the United States, **Toshiko Takaezu** was born in Pepeekeo, Hawaii in 1922; she began studying ceramics, along with design and weaving, at the University of Hawaii from 1948 to 1951. The year she finished her studies, Takaezu left for the mainland armed with a supply of black sand from the beaches of Hawaii to incorporate into her work, and she enrolled in courses at the Cranbrook Academy of Art in Bloomfield Hills, Michigan. At Cranbrook, Takaezu studied sculpture with William McVey, but Finnish ceramics artist Maija Grotell, who also taught at Cranbrook, had the strongest influence on the emerging artist. Grotell's emphasis on mastery of technique, her unwavering belied that ceramics could be art, and her careful respect for the individuality of her students enabled Takaezu to find her own distinct approach to the medium.

The emergence of Takaezu's career coincided with the ascendancy in the United States and Canada of the philosophies and aesthetics of the Japanese ceramics folk art movement. In 1926, philosopher Yanagi Soetsu in Japan advocated a return to traditional methods of firing and glazing clay partly as a response to Japan's increased industrialization; his ideas were circulated in the West through Bernard Leach's *A Potter's Book*. Takaezu read Leach's book, and during his lecture tour in the early 1950s, she met Leach as well as potter Hamada Shoji and Soetsu, who had become the director of the National Folk Art Museum of Japan.

In 1954, Takaezu graduated from Cranbrook, and the following year, she spent eight months in Japan, living in a Zen Buddhist temple and studying the tea ceremony central to traditional Japanese ceramics and the folk art movement. During this time, she met other prominent ceramics artists in the country, including Kitaoji Rosanjin and Kaneshige Toyo. Upon her return to the United States in 1956, Takaezu began teaching in the ceramics department at Cleveland Institute of Art, where she was a faculty member until 1964. Soon after, her work underwent a radical shift. In 1958, she began creating thrown forms that were almost completely closed, except for "a vestigial reminder of their functional origin . . . a small, roughly finished opening at the top."[†] These works would soon become the elongated, richly textured, rounded sculptures that are instantly recognizable as Takaezu's work.

The development of larger kilns in the ceramics world enabled Takaezu to increase the scale of her work, which sometimes reached over sixty inches, as in her *Tree* series of the 1970s. While critics have often discussed her work in relation to Japan and Eastern approaches to art-making, Takaezu's practice of applying pigment and glaze by pouring, dripping, or brushing, and even finger-painting it owes as much to action painting and abstract expressionism, as Darrel Sewell has observed. Her process of acting upon the clay combined with her mastery of throwing and firing techniques produces visually complex works with enormous tactile appeal.[‡]

Throughout her career, Takaezu has been an active teacher and the recipient of numerous honors. In 1964, she received a Louis Comfort Tiffany Foundation grant and a Craftsman's Fellowship from the National Endowment for the Arts in 1980. She holds honorary doctorates from the Moore College of Art and Design (Philadelphia), University of Hawaii at Honolulu, and Princeton University, where she was a member of the visual arts faculty from 1967 to 1992. In 1990, the Montclair Art Museum (New Jersey) mounted the retrospective *Toshiko Takaezu: Four Decades,* which traveled for two years, and another retrospective in 1995 traveled throughout Japan and the United States.

* Toshiko Takaezu, "Toshiko Takaezu: A Thrown Form," *Ceramic Monthly* (November 1975), 34. Quoted in Darrel Sewell, *The Poetry of Clay: The Art of Toshiko Takaezu,* exh. cat., Philadelphia Museum of Art, August 7, 2004–March 6, 2005, 5.

† Sewell, 5.

‡ Sewell, 6.

TOSHIKO TAKAEZU (B.1922), *UNTITLED,* C.1965, GLAZED STONEWARE, 12 X 8 X 7 INCHES

LEFT TO RIGHT:

TOSHIKO TAKAEZU (B.1922), *UNTITLED*, C.1965, GLAZED STONEWARE, 21 X 12 X 12 INCHES, SIGNED

TOSHIKO TAKAEZU (B.1922), *UNTITLED*, C.1965, GLAZED STONEWARE, 16 X 17 X 17 INCHES

TOSHIKO TAKAEZU (B.1922), *UNTITLED*, C.1960, GLAZED STONEWARE, 21 X 10 X 10 INCHES

TOSHIKO TAKAEZU (B.1922), *UNTITLED*, C.1965, GLAZED STONEWARE, 18 X 12 X 12 INCHES, SIGNED

128

I BRUSH COLOR ON TO VIOLATE THE FORM, AND IT COMES OUT A COMPLETE NEW THING, WHICH INVOLVES A PAINTING CONCEPT ON A THREE-DIMENSIONAL SURFACE, A NEW IDEA. THESE THINGS ARE EXPLODING, JUMPING OFF. I WANTED TO PICK UP ON THAT ENERGY. THAT'S DIFFERENT FROM DECORATING THE SURFACE, WHICH ENHANCES FORM . . . . I WANTED TO CHANGE THE FORM, GET MORE EXCITEMENT GOING.*

PETER VOULKOS 1924-2002

Born in Bozeman, Montana in 1924, **Peter Voulkos** was one of five children in his close-knit family. His parents were Greek immigrants, and during the Depression, Voulkos held several jobs in order to help the family survive. In 1942, Voulkos finished high school and made his way to Oregon, where he found work making floor molds for engine castings and casting iron fittings for American Liberty ships. In 1943, he was drafted into the US Army Air Corps and spent most of the war in the Pacific theater. With funding from the GI Bill, Voulkos enrolled in courses at Montana State College (now University) in his hometown of Bozeman after the war. In 1951, he received his bachelor's degree and used the remainder of his GI Bill funding to earn a Master of Fine Arts degree from the California College of Arts and Crafts in Oakland, which he completed in 1952. That same year, Voulkos participated in his first gallery exhibition, and in 1953, he traveled to New York, where he frequented the Club and the Cedar Tavern, meeting artists such as Franz Kline, Jack Tworkov, Philip Guston, and Robert Rauschenberg. That same year, Voulkos's sculpture was included in two important New York exhibitions—*Good Design* at the Museum of Modern Art (MoMA) and *Designer Craftsmen, USA 1953* at the Brooklyn Museum, where he was awarded the juried exhibition's top prize. In 1954, he began teaching at the Los Angeles County Art Institute (now Otis), where he eventually established a ceramics department.

In the mid-1950s, after his time in New York, Voulkos began to move away from the throwing and glazing skills he had perfected as a student. Embracing abstract expressionism's emphasis on the gestural in art, Voulkos attempted to make room for the spontaneous in ceramic sculpture, marking, altering, and destroying his works to produce new forms. By 1958, he was creating work on a much larger scale, assembling wheel-thrown pottery elements into eight-foot constructions that he coated with an epoxy resin, turning the artwork itself into an analysis of the process of pottery-making. Voulkos's radical deconstruction of the traditional ceramics process and form would inspire countless ceramicists who followed, but in 1959, the iconoclastic thrust of his work disturbed the conservative administration at the LA County Art Institute, and he was fired from teaching there.

Undaunted, Voulkos continued to explore new approaches to sculpture as his career continued to rise. In 1960, Peter Selz curated an exhibition of his work for the Penthouse Gallery at MoMA, and Voulkos began to work in bronze, opening a foundry in Berkeley with fellow University of California Berkeley faculty members Don Haskin and Harold Paris. Voulkos's bronze works were even greater in scale than his ceramics, and at the end of the decade, he created *Mr. Ishi,* an eighteen-by-forty-foot bronze work commissioned by the Oakland Museum.

Like Toshiko Takaezu, Voulkos had been greatly influenced by the Japanese folk art movement. He had read Bernard Leach's *A Potter's Book* and had also met Hamada Shoji and Yanagi Soetsu during Leach's lecture tour. This interest endured throughout Voulkos's career, and in 1979, he made a series of plates fired in an *anagama,* a Japanese wood-fired kiln, which operates at high temperatures, producing a richly textured surface. During the last two decades of his life, Voulkos made most of his pottery in public, at demonstrations throughout the United States and Japan.

Possibly more than any other artist, Voulkos had a tremendous impact on ceramics art, creating "a vocabulary of actions and forms that are now fixed in the language of contemporary clay, including 'passthroughs' (knobs of porcelain pushed through a stoneware piece from the back), stacks (…tiered, chimney-shaped structures of thick clay …), and ice buckets (short, thick, squarish containers, always cracked)."[†]

* Peter Voulkos, quoted by Rose Slivka, "The Artist and His Work: Risk and Revelation," Rose Slivka and Karen Tsujimoto *The Art of Peter Voulkos,* exh. cat., Oakland Museum and Kodansha International, 1995, 49.

† Janet Koplos, "Peter Voulkos, 1924-2002—ceramic sculptor—Obituary," *Art in America,* April 2002. http://findarticles.com/p/articles/mi_m1248/is_4_90/ai_84669384/pg_2/ (accessed July 2009).

PETER VOULKOS (1924-2002), *UNTITLED,* 1955-56, GLAZED CERAMIC, 31 1/2 X 19 1/2 X 19 1/2 INCHES, SIGNED

EXHIBITION CHECKLIST
PART I: PAINTING

© 2009 The New York Times

NEW YORK, FRIDAY, JULY 10, 2009

The Shock of the New, 50 Years On

BY ROBERTA SMITH

What did they get and when did they get it? This is a good if possibly superficial yardstick for measuring museums' alertness to new art. After auction prices, it may be the closest the art world gets to baseball stats. If a work of art in a public collection withstands the so-called tests of time, the gap between when it was made and when it was acquired becomes a telling and sometimes thrilling bit of data, like a high batting average. The shorter the interval, the greater the sense of institutional nerve and prescience.

In "The Sweeney Decade: The 1959 Inaugural," at the Guggenheim Museum, the interval is always short. Of the 24 paintings and sculptures on view, all were made in the 1950s and acquired during that decade, usually within a year or two of their creation. Some are still interesting, others not; but they reveal a museum trying to sniff out the new and unafraid to put its money where its curatorial instincts pointed, albeit at 1950s prices.

The exhibition also demonstrates that these instincts are never infallible, a point that is nicely expanded on by a coincidental but oddly complementary show of the same size at the Michael Rosenfeld Gallery. Many of its 25 paintings from the 1950s and '60s are by artists who were not on museums' radar at the time.

"The Sweeney Decade" is part of the Guggenheim's celebration of the 50th anniversary of its Frank Lloyd Wright building. It honors James Johnson Sweeney, who was the museum's second director, from 1952 until 1960 (an eight-year decade actually). Sweeney oversaw the construction of the Wright building and broadened the Guggenheim's acquisitions beyond the mostly European, mostly nonobjective art favored by Hilla Rebay, his predecessor.

Sweeney acquired work by European modernists who had fallen outside Rebay's nonobjective parameters - Brancusi being one. He also set his sights on younger postwar artists from Asia and the United States, often buying directly from the studio. And he organized the inaugural exhibition in Wright's new building, which consisted of 133 works, according to its ancient typed checklist.

A hundred and one were by well-known European modernists, with special emphasis on Wassily Kandinsky (23 paintings), whom Rebay considered the lodestar of nonobjective art. The remaining 32 were Sweeney acquisitions; 15 of them are in the current show.

It's too bad there wasn't room for more, but "The Sweeney Decade" still constitutes a fascinating time capsule in its combined distillation of a curator's taste, a museum's optimism and a historical moment. It is also a snapshot of the way postwar artists strove to be innovative, or at least up to date, in their emphasis on the materials and processes of painting.

I can't say the canon is overturned: the strongest works here are by two of its stalwarts. One is Jackson Pollock's 1953 "Ocean Greyness," whose nodes of color embedded in thrashing strokes of black and gray create a field of oculuslike openings that presage Lee Bontecou's canvas reliefs. The other is Willem de Kooning's "Composition," from 1955, an equally dense expanse of clashing brushstrokes, with red dominant. In contrast, many noncanonical painters look as misguided as they ever have, among them Hans Hartung, Jean-Pierre Riopelle and Antonio Saura.

But some unfamiliar artworks command attention. With its garish color and emphatic brushwork, Karel Appel's totemic 1953 "Two Heads" (acquired in 1954) points to the work of Jean-Michel Basquiat and may also have been grist for Picasso's relentless mill. Takeo Yamaguchi's boldly scaled 1958 "Work — Yellow" is dominated by a lopsided double square of deep yellow. Applied with palette knife in a thick, smooth slab - a method that Brice Marden would soon adopt - it occupies a subtly rhythmic field of thinner brown brushwork, evoking both the calligraphy and the sword hilts of Japan.

The British sculptor Eduardo Paolozzi's "St. Sebastian, No. 2," from 1958, teeters between postwar existentialism and Pop appropriation, and between traditional bronze and assemblage. It seems nearly every part of the figure is cast from a different made or found element. It becomes dizzying to try to figure out which is which and how it was all put together.

In her selections for this show Tracey Bashkoff, the Guggenheim's associate curator for collections and exhibitions, has stressed the international sweep of Sweeney's vision and the unfamiliar parts of the collection. That may explain why Franz Kline and Stuart Davis are not here, although both were represented in the inaugural show with canvases that outclass quite a bit that is. But I was happy to become acquainted with the paintings of Luis Feito and Alfred Manessier and the sculptures of Eduardo Chillida, David Hayes and Etienne Hajdu.

In the corner of one gallery the desire to get beyond painting's conventional gestures and materials is evident in the efforts of Antoni Tapies (lots of sand), Alberto Burri (burnt wood) and Conrad Marca-Relli (canvas shapes on canvas). They call attention to like-minded artists whose work Sweeney did not acquire: Lucio Fontana, Yves Klein, Ms. Bontecou and John Chamberlain, as well as Jasper Johns.

At the Rosenfeld gallery "Abstract Expressionism: Further Evidence (Part 1: Painting)" includes a slightly different cast of characters. Although there are two artists from the Guggenheim show (James Brooks and Marca-Relli), and a few others who were highly visible players in the '50s (Hans Hofmann, Joan Mitchell and Milton Resnick), many of the artists here were not being snapped up by museums. Painters like Norman Lewis, Jay DeFeo, Charles Seliger, Charles Alston and Alma Thomas report from an Abstract Expressionist road less traveled.

It is instructive to cherry-pick from this ensemble, with an eye to what might both shake up and enhance the Sweeney show. My choices from the pre-1960 works include the 1951 Brooks painting (it's better than the Guggenheim's 1958 canvas); Alfred Leslie's monstrous "Hoboken Collage" (1953-54); Mr. Resnick's somber but beautifully painted "A," from 1957; and two Alfonso Ossorio paintings, but especially the oozing relieflike "Mirror Point" (1958), which describes a tree trunk with thin sheets of knotty wood stuck in the thick paint.

But the work that should go to the Guggenheim or some other public collection before all others is Beauford Delaney's "Composition 16," from 1954-56, a shimmering field of dark, green-tinged yellow laid over a field of finely minced primaries and finished with a series of flat ribbonlike brushstrokes—also yellow—whose meandering lines seem vaguely floral.

Reflecting Delaney's admiration for Monet and possibly an awareness of Pollock, this marvelous painting is a must-have for any museum that wants to expand its definition of Abstract Expressionism beyond the white men who still dominate it.

"The Sweeney Decade: Acquisitions of the 1959 Inaugural" continues through Sept. 2 at the Guggenheim Museum, 1071 Fifth Avenue, at 89th Street; (212) 423-3500. "Abstract Expressionism: Further Evidence (Part 1: Painting)" continues through July 31 at the Michael Rosenfeld Gallery, 24 West 57th Street, Manhattan; (212) 247-0082.

$\mathscr{E}$XHIBITION $\mathscr{C}$HECKLIST
PART II: SCULPTURE

p.73   Robert Arneson (1930-1992)
        Untitled, c.1959
        glazed ceramic
        13 1/2 x 8 1/2 x 8 inches, signed

p.75   Robert Arneson (1930-1992)
        Untitled (Coiled Pot), 1961
        glazed ceramic
        25 1/2 x 12 x 12 inches

p.77   Lee Bontecou (b.1931)
        Untitled, 1963
        welded steel and paint
        21 1/2 x 31 1/4 x 6 1/2 inches, signed

p.79   Louise Bourgeois (b.1911)
        Untitled, 1953
        bronze with black patina and steel base
        Edition 1/6
        51 x 8 1/2 x 4 inches, signed

p.81   John Chamberlain (b.1927)
        Untitled, 1961
        painted metal
        5 x 4 x 3 1/2 inches
        Private Collection
        Courtesy of Anthony Meier Fine Arts

p.85   Harold Cousins (1916-1992)
        La Forêt, c.1960
        welded bronze with patina on
        wood base
        42 x 47 1/2 x 17 1/2 inches

p.83   Harold Cousins (1916-1992)
        Plaiton Suspendu (Hanging Plaiton),
        1958
        welded steel and brass with patina
        59 x 17 x 11 inches

p.87   Dorothy Dehner (1901-1994)
        Long Landscape, 1961
        bronze with patina
        47 x 6 x 2 1/2 inches

p.89   Dorothy Dehner (1901-1994)
        Untitled (Mask), 1961
        bronze with patina
        15 3/8 x 11 1/2 x 3 1/2 inches, signed

p.93   Claire Falkenstein (1908-1997)
        Untitled (Element #2), c.1965
        copper and glass
        11 1/2 x 16 x 15 inches

p.91   Claire Falkenstein (1908-1997)
        Untitled (Sun), 1960
        nickel plated steel
        34 x 56 x 13 inches

p.95   Herbert Ferber (1906-1991)
        Calligraphic Mercury II, 1955
        brazed brass on wood base
        50 3/4 x 40 x 16 inches, signed

p.97   David Hare (1917-1992)
        Leda's Dream of the Swan, 1960
        bronze and steel
        59 1/2 x 23 x 19 inches

p.99   Richard Hunt (b.1935)
        Untitled, 1961
        copper, brass, patina and paint
        18 1/2 x 12 x 8 3/4 inches, signed

p.101   Ibram Lassaw (1913-2003)
        Sirius, 1951
        bronze over galvanized wire
        21 1/2 x 22 x 17 inches

p.103   Seymour Lipton (1903-1986)
        Invocation #2, 1949
        lead and iron with artist's wood base
        87 1/2 x 13 x 13 inches